PULLING LEVERS

PULLING LEVERS

**BUILDING AN INSPIRED CULTURE AND
DRIVING WINNING RESULTS THROUGH
FOCUS ON THE FOUR PS**

Jim Lipuma

ISBN-13: 9781533512574
ISBN-10: 1533512574
Library of Congress Control Number: 2016910035
CreateSpace Independent Publishing Platform
North Charleston, South Carolina

This book is dedicated to my amazing family, who provide unconditional love, undying support, and deep inspiration every day and in every way.

In addition, I'd like to dedicate this book to those mentors who had a direct and long-lasting impact on my professional career and personal life. Thank you, Bob, Dan, Peter, Chris, Cary, and Mark.

CONTENTS

INTRODUCTION

Culture, in its most pure societal sense, can be defined as socially derived, taken-for-granted assumptions about how to think and act. Further, societal culture involves beliefs and values about what is desirable and undesirable in a community of people and a set of formal or informal practices to support the value. Somewhat cold and clinical, isn't it?

What comes to mind when I mention the countries of Russia, North Korea, or even the United States? So much has to do with our experiences and impressions, which have largely been shaped by media, those countries' leaders, and our own personal biases and prejudices. Imagine attempting to alter the impressions you have of the examples I provided. It would be a difficult "ask," as you likely have a deep opinion on each at this point in your life. Now, what if there were an election or coup and the leaders changed within each of the examples, placing a more positive-minded leader in the role? My bet is that your opinion or hope for the future might change.

The point of this example is to call out that leadership has an impact on your perceptions of a given culture, as the leader can set the tone for, alter the vision of, impact the values of, and guide a society. Whether in society or business, the person in charge has a great and profound responsibility to the brand and culture that will be created as a result of his or her leadership. Talk about a heavy burden!

In more than thirty years of leadership, I have had the opportunity to be a part of several best-in-class companies and cultures. They were inclusive. They were purpose driven. Our values aligned. It felt good. It felt right.

In a recent study conducted by Deloitte (2016 Deloitte Human Capital Trends), the research identified that only 19 percent of professionals say their companies possess the right corporate culture. Only 19 percent! Said another way, 81 percent feel that their companies do not possess the right corporate culture. Imagine what would happen to our economy if 81 percent of employees felt that their company *did* embody the proper culture. My guess is that we would have employee churn at a record low and employee output at a record high. What impact might this have on our economy? Well, there are companies that are doing just that.

Annually, there are companies that consistently sit atop *Fortune* magazine's "Best Places to Work" list. In fact, Zappos has sat in this ranking consistently since 2009, with 82 percent of its employees stating that their workplace is great. In addition, take a look at these internal employee grades:

- Ninety-four percent—People celebrate special events around here.

- Ninety-three percent—I am able to take time off from work when I think it is necessary.
- Ninety-two percent—We have special and unique benefits here.
- Ninety-one percent—I feel good about the way we contribute to the community.
- Ninety-one percent—I can be myself around here.

Having toured the facility, I can attest to the fact that the culture is amazing. As I mentioned earlier, it begins at the top. I'd like to share a quote from Tony Hsieh, CEO of Zappos. I think this pretty much sums it up.

For me, my role is about unleashing what people already have inside them that is maybe supressed in most work environments.

—Tony Hsieh

There has been much research on why employees stay with a company and why they leave. In most studies, there are consistent key elements. Employees who stay state that they are challenged, involved, empowered, appreciated, valued, trusted, mentored, and on a mission. They also state that they are paid well and promoted but overwhelmingly, people stay due to intrinsic rewards. It is seen time and time again: *why we work determines how well we work.*

When I decided to write this book, I reflected on my experiences and kept coming back to the four Ps that have been at the core of my career and instrumental in building an enviable culture—People, Passion, Proposition, and Process. Each of these areas requires keen and committed focus at all levels and within all channels. It's not easy to create a winning culture, but it is possible with the right dedication and focus.

Creating a passionate and enviable culture takes full commitment. Each of the four Ps is critical. An unbalanced approach will create imbalance. As an example, if there is a disproportionate amount of focus on the process, the organization could skew too far right and be viewed as a tight, robotic, and micromanaged organization. Too skewed toward the people side and accountability could be lacking. Creating a powerful culture takes equal commitment to all four areas, as each area plays a critical role in the desired outcome. I have a big goal when I enter an organization. I want my company to be viewed as a "Top Place to Work." If you commit to the four Ps and remain focused on them consistently, this dream can become a reality. This is all about committing to your people, igniting a passion within, internalizing the proposition, and implementing a repeatable process that will lead to predictable results. Consider each a lever: when all levers are pulled equally and with unwavering commitment, the engine hums.

The title of this book is derived from a common phrase used in business. *Pulling levers* often refers to identifying the key components that, when pulled properly, have a direct and substantive impact on the business. The four Ps are levers, but there are many levers within each of these critical areas. We will discuss the many levers within business throughout the book. When approached correctly, pulling the right levers in the right way will change the trajectory of your business forever.

SECTION 1: PEOPLE

When you complete this section, you will be able to

1. gain a fresh perspective on your team, identifying those who are moving the vision forward as well as those who are fighting the current;
2. have a plan to identify, befriend, and win over the top performers, ensuring alignment and full support for the vision;
3. build the "brand" that you envision for your business; and
4. embrace the need to make necessary (but tough) calls around personnel.

No company, small or large, can win over the long run without energized employees who believe in the mission and understand how to achieve it.

—Jack Welch

I n 1954, in the small town of Milan, Indiana, (population 1,100) stood a school of 161 students, made up of 88 girls and 73 boys. Ten boys made the basketball team and set out on an unprecedented journey to shape history.

Indiana is a state that prides itself on basketball above all else. Texas has football, and Indiana has basketball. This team from rural Indiana accomplished the unthinkable. Milan won the high school state basketball championship in 1954, against all odds, with a story that was brought to life in the film *Hoosiers* in 1986.

I use the phrase *against all odds*, as most people have a tendency to give the odds-on victory to those with the numbers. It is assumed that a school with more students would have a better probability of a positive outcome. It's simple math. What this strategy fails to take into consideration are the skill and the will of the people involved. If you have the right talent coupled with the right passion, will, grit, and commitment, great things will happen. Success has very little to do with the size of the person or team and everything to do with individual makeup and collective resolve. As the old saying goes, "It's not the size of the dog in the fight, but the size of the fight in the dog." At the end of the day, it's what's inside that ultimately determines the outcome.

As we begin the first section, we address the most important P in the four Ps: people. In a previous role, I reported to a manager who was keenly bright and deliberately systematic in his approach. He described himself as lacking "people skills." A senior leader who lacks a focus on people will ultimately be unable to get the absolute most out of his or her people. While building automation and focusing on consistency in process are both critical factors in the success of an organization, understanding that the people are the engine that moves the machine must be paramount to a leader's way of thinking. Leadership is about identifying talent, pulling the best out, and tightly aligning everyone to a common purpose. This is imperative number one. With amazing people come amazing results. The difference between best-in-class organizations and mediocre companies boils down to the individual strength and the overall character of the organization. The best and most admired organizations focus intently on bringing together talented people who share a desire to be the best, do the best, and build something truly special. The best people understand their place and their role and understand that it is through their individual contributions that the organization will succeed. Above all else, as a senior leader of an organization, you must embrace the fact that the ultimate success of your organization resides in your ability to identify the absolute best talent and nurture that talent to surpass their own personal expectations. Find people who don't know what they can't do. Without self-imposed limitations, anything is possible.

Identifying talent is not an easy task, but as a leader, this must be your top priority. Nothing is as important as the people with whom you choose to stand side by side in your company. Your ultimate success or failure lies in your ability to be great at finding talent.

CHAPTER 1

DEFINE THE ATTRIBUTES YOU SEEK

B ack in 2014, I wrote a book entitled *Lead from the Front: 101 Leadership Quips, Quotes, and Anecdotes That Will Impact Your Career and Your Life*. In that book, anecdote number one is "Lead from the Front," anecdote number two is "You Work for Your Family," and anecdote number three is "It's All About the People." While the book was not intended to sequentially rank order all 101, in retrospect, had I rank ordered them, anecdote number three is right where it needs to be.

The absolute most important factor in the success of an organization, above all else, lies in identifying, developing, and unleashing talent. This section is completely committed to doing just that and doing it right. An organization should make lots of mistakes, or it is not taking enough shots. We should be testing, learning, and perfecting our product, pricing, approach, outreach, etc. At all costs, we need to be diligent about getting hiring spot on. While far from easy, it is essential. This begins with defining the attributes you seek.

Over the years, I have made hiring talent my priority and my personal quest. Through research, testing, and being personally involved in nearly every hire within my business, over the past ten-plus years, I have narrowed down the qualities and attributes that I seek. This is the first step in accomplished hiring. While I have specifically mentioned recruitment here, these qualities stand for current employees as well.

- **Good person**—In the first five minutes, you can tell if someone is a good person. Notice the way he or she engages with and treats other people and the way he or she approaches you in that first engagement. Is she looking you in the eyes? Is he smiling? Does it feel genuine? Does the person you are interviewing care about what you are saying, and is he or she active in his or her listening? Good people will bring their hearts to the organization and will be respectful throughout.
- **Humble**—Look for people who, when asked about their accomplishments, are credit givers rather than credit takers. In an interview, I give a certain amount of leeway, as this is the applicant's moment to take credit and tell his or her story. He or she is trying to get the job, so he or she should be in "sell" mode. Look for people who are humble, who pass credit to others, and who are confident about who they are and comfortable passing credit to others.
- **Grateful**—Grateful people make amazing employees because they appreciate what they have and share that openly with others. Nothing fosters a healthy

culture quite like grateful employees. There is an energy around those who are grateful.

- **High EQ**—"Emotional quotient" involves the capacity for people to recognize their own emotions, as well as those of other people, and to have the ability to discriminate among feelings and label them appropriately. It also guides thinking and behavior. In my world, a high emotional quotient trumps a high intelligence quotient. Those employees in tune with their feelings, as well as the feelings of others, tend to be a bit more measured in their reactions to people and situations.

- **Outward thinker**—I look for people who, in line with having a high EQ, think and act in the best interest of others, as opposed to the best interests of themselves. An organization is healthy when people look at the greater good and focus on the betterment of those in their personal or professional community.

- **Intellectually curious**—Look for people who are interested in expanding their breadth of knowledge and who really want to understand how things work and the potential that lies ahead. These are the people who will drive innovation for your organization. Look for those who ask questions and bring forward ideas and solutions.

- **Passionate**—At the core of a successful person lies an innate desire to help create and to be a part of something special. Passion fuels success. Passion is an absolute must-have attribute.

- **Driven**—In order to foster a success-minded organization, we must have success-driven employees.

An organization made up of passionate and driven employees is 80 percent of the way to success. I read a quote once that stated, "Someone once told me not to bite off more than I can chew. I told them I would rather choke on greatness than nibble on mediocrity."

- **Optimistic**—We hear the word *no* far more often than we hear the word *yes*, especially in a sales environment. We must surround ourselves with people who see the opportunity in the difficulty and the path as the adventure. Harry Truman once said, "A pessimist is one who makes difficulties of his opportunities, and an optimist is one who makes opportunities of his difficulties."

- **Trustworthy**—At the center of a healthy relationship sits trust, and trust is more evident in actions than in words. Look for people who embrace the vision and crown the company. Look for those who prioritize the needs of their clients and organization above their own personal needs. Find people who understand that good comes to those who commit to the mission and the organization, above all else.

In section 4, we will discuss interview questions, exercises, and testing that allow the leader to best identify these critical attributes and traits.

CHAPTER 2

DETERMINE YOUR "BRAND"

B ack in 2011, Harry Beckwith published a book titled *You, Inc.* As you might imagine, the book was about the brand that you create for yourself, as you truly are a brand. This chapter will ask you to dig deep and determine how you would like to be perceived. Marketers have to make determinations around their target audiences, their pricing models, their uniqueness, and their fit; as a leader, you must do the same.

At the beginning of *Pulling Levers*, I asked you to think about how you felt when I mentioned Russia. Today, Russia's president is Vladimir Putin. Think about his personal brand for a minute. It is based on force, strength of purpose, and conformity. There is very little room for opinion or democracy. Putin has the ability to alter that perception (or reality), but he is comfortable and confident in the brand that he has created. Right or wrong, that is a choice that he has made. I realize that this is an extreme example, but as the leader of an organization, you have the opportunity to develop your own brand as you, too, see fit. I tell all of my new-hire classes the same thing I told my daughters when they went off to college: Nobody cares what you have done in your past. At this moment, you have the opportunity to become whomever you want to become. It is a choice that you have the ability and responsibility to make.

In determining your personal brand, you must start by planting your flag and articulating what you stand for. As the old saying goes, "If you don't stand for something, you will fall for anything." Much like a politician, you need a platform that clearly spells out what you stand for, what you believe in, what you expect, and what expectations you place on yourself, your people, and your organization. You need to share beliefs, boundaries, and your vision. People will follow leaders who have a platform, who confidently state their positions, and who possess a clarity for the road ahead. By way of an example, I will share my personal brand platform. I am consistent and unwavering in application:

1. I believe in and invest in my people.
2. I will stand behind my people and support them, as long as they have the best interests of our constituents in mind.
3. I will create an inclusive environment, which will foster an understanding that every opinion counts and matters. I believe that those closest to our clients should be responsible for the path we travel. We will build and shape our organization together.
4. I believe that in order to "get," we must also "give." Each person will be expected to give his or her all to his or her role, to those whom he or she serves, and to his or her organization, and I expect nothing less

than a successful outcome. In exchange, employees will be involved, engaged, challenged, appreciated, respected, and well paid.

5. We will practice full transparency in our organization. What I know, you will know. No surprises.

6. We will foster a healthy competitiveness in our company. We will support one another while striving to be one dollar better, rather than winning at the expense of others.

7. We will become a "Best Place to Work" in our city, and as we continue to grow, we will end up on *Fortune*'s annual announcement of "Best Places to Work."

8. We will challenge one another to think in new ways and to reinvent our organization in ways we never thought possible.

9. We will win by implementing standards and expectations that allow us to grow, and we will develop our internal talent and hire exceptional outside talent, who will allow us to continue to build upon our exceptional culture.

Take time and determine what you believe in, stand for, and want to represent. Write it down, and share it for all to see. Review it often, and continue to keep it front and center in your team discussions. Openness in communication leads to trust, respect, unity, and an amazing culture.

CHAPTER 3

UNDERSTAND WHAT YOU HAVE OR WHAT YOU ARE INHERITING

Whether I'm inheriting an operation or already in the seat, I am a firm believer in consistently surveying my business. I ask the important questions, and I do it in a confidential way, so that people can have a voice and avoid any considerations around reprisal or retribution. I want to understand where we stand, where we are excelling, where we are falling short, and where we have blind spots. The key is to ask qualifying questions up front, so you can attribute responses to channels. This will help identify if your successes or challenges are organization-wide or isolated to particular divisions. Please understand, this is not about catching anyone doing something wrong. This is about identifying issues and opportunities that can have a profound impact on the organization as a whole.

As part of my pre-onboarding into a new organization, I send out a survey. In that survey, I ask between twenty and twenty-five questions. I like to focus on themes that lead to healthy corporate cultures. Here are several questions that I use consistently:

- **Communication**—On a scale of one to ten (ten being best), how would you grade our overall communication?
- **Peer talent**—On a scale of one to ten (ten being best), how would you rate the talent of your coworkers?
- **Leadership talent**—On a scale of one to ten (ten being best), how would you rate the talent of your supervisor?
- **Culture**—On a scale of one to ten (ten being best), how would you rate the overall environment?
- **Happiness**—On a scale of one to ten (ten being best), how happy are you at our organization?
- **Passion**—Are you passionate about what we do? Yes/No.
- **Vision**—Are you clear on our vision and where we are heading? Yes/No.
- **Investment in them personally**—How do you feel about the level of professional development that you receive? Very high, high, moderate, low.
- **Value**—Do you believe in the value that we bring to our clients? Very high, high, moderate, low.
- **Pride**—What is your level of pride when you tell your friends that you work at our organization? Very high, high, moderate, low.

You should also incorporate ten-plus questions that are very specific to potential needs that you have identified, so you can determine if there is an appetite. Additionally, you should have several open-ended questions, which will help to identify potential product, service, or offering opportunities. This will help in building your plan of attack.

The absolute key here is to assess the findings and put together a presentation, which you will roll out to the entire organization that you represent. A survey without disclosure and a follow-on plan is useless and will drive a level of distrust around the motives of the survey. You must be transparent on the findings, the assessment, and the plan that will ensue as a result. You can then prioritize the findings and develop/nominate teams to begin dissection, solution, design, and potential implementation. The survey provides a foundation from which to build the overarching plan that everyone has had a hand in developing.

As a result of surveying, there may be things that you are not prepared to address, change, or introduce. I would highly recommend that you address these. By addressing them, you are living by your personal commitment to transparency. Open communication does not mean people get what they want. Transparency calls for listening, understanding, and addressing, and that's it. At the end of the day, you are the leader, and you have a responsibility to run the business. Transparency allows you to be open and honest about both the whys and the why nots. Being a good leader and creating a strong culture call for strength and conviction, while being completely wide open to new ideas that will propel the business forward. Surveying your team often will allow you to assess advancement or retreat, while understanding and potentially implementing ideas that surface from those closest to the needs of your end users.

CHAPTER 4

LOCATE THE BEST AND BEFRIEND THEM

A ssume that you are currently leading a team of people. How close are you to your best people? Do you have a relationship that spans beyond standard communications with all employees? If you are new to an organization, have you determined the best employees? Have you done this solely subjectively, via feedback from others, or have you placed an objective view toward this exercise as well? In both scenarios, it is imperative that you align yourself with the best people—and fast. If your best people support the values, embrace the vision, are seen as leaders among their peers, and consistently overdeliver on expectations, I'd recommend that you get really close with them, really quickly.

Whenever I enter a new organization, after the initial survey, I ask for feedback on each employee directly from his or her supervisor and within each level of the organization. If you run a large organization, look two or three levels downstream. I also identify all key performance indicators (KPIs) by group and build out a ranking system, plotting all peers within their respective groups. We will discuss the ranking process later in the book, but for now I will keep the procedure at a high level.

By ranking all peers, you marry science with art. By relying solely on feedback from employees/leaders, you will have a tendency to skew toward art (feelings/subjective) over science (math/objective). Facts are our friends, and while there is a place for subjectivity, it takes a back seat to being objective in our analysis. Coming fresh into an organization allows you to eliminate bias in your assessment. An additional step would be to ask for previous performance reviews, if the organization uses this process as standard protocol. Once you've statistically ranked the talent, begin the subjective process. Without sharing the ranking, ask the supervisors to rank their people, best to worst. Leave it open ended, and see how they go about assessing and sharing their findings/opinions. It will tell you a lot about that supervisor. The goal of involving each supervisor is to confirm that someone shares the values and aligns well with the organization from both a personality and a cultural standpoint. When you have this, move to the next step.

Set up one-on-one time with each of several top performers within each peer group. You will have goals entering into these sessions:

1. You want to get to know them and understand their personal vision, values, and goals.
2. You want them to get to know you, so that they can understand your vision, values, and goals.
3. You want to ask open-ended questions, in order to assess their curiosity, thought processes, passion for the organization, and intellect.
4. You want to form a bond and an alignment.

5. You want to build trust.
6. You want to have allies.

Top performers who align with the vision and values of the company could potentially end up being a part of your leadership team. At a minimum, they will support the organization (and you) outwardly, and that is a critical need to avoid an "us versus them" scenario. You will be making changes, and unless you have internal support from people respected on the front lines, you will meet resistance. I would argue that the credibility that comes from a respected peer would rival (and potentially trump) that of a supervisor or CEO. People look beyond their leaders for affirmation. People will look to their peers and will flex as they flex. Earning the support and respect of your key players will go a long way in ensuring alignment of the entire organization.

There is a fine line here that I'd like to address. You must be careful not to place these peer leaders on too great of a pedestal, comparing them to others within their peer groups. As much as you will want to use them to build best practices, you have to be sensitive and share that throne. If you highlight a particular individual too much, it could backfire on you, driving a wedge between your peer leaders and their peers. Again, it's a fine line. Walk up to the line, but don't go over it.

Later in the book, we will discuss a couple of ways that you can recognize and leverage these talented employees but for now, here are a few ideas:

- They become part of a formal mentoring program.
- They are part of an employee council that you initiate. They potentially "chair" the council.

- They become part of a leadership development program.
- They have a direct line to you, and you to them, to share ideas and brainstorm potential opportunities facing the organization.
- They will be in the comparison set of the personality profile assessment for future hires.

Identifying the best internal talent and befriending them is paramount to driving a culture that influences all people within your organization. Use this piece of the process to your advantage—you'll need it.

CHAPTER 5

FIND/CREATE MORE LIKE THE BEST

In a traditional organization, you will have A, B, and C performers. Your A performers are those who consistently overdeliver on goals, possess the intellect and curiosity to shape the path and future, live the values, and openly support the mission. They make up roughly 20 percent of your workforce. Members of the A team have the greatest potential to do more with what they have. They are also the most likely to be recruited and, potentially, to leave. As discussed in the last chapter, engage them, value them, challenge them, recognize them, and reward them.

B players make up roughly 60 percent of your team. They are most likely to be the ones who carry internal "history" with them. They do their work yet are seldom recognized as top performers or overachievers. An opportunity exists here. Many times, B players are past A players who have lost a level of faith or have outside influences today that might not have been there previously (children, other priorities). There may also be an alignment issue. In other words, placing them in roles better suited for their skill sets or moving them to different supervisors could lift them to A ranks.

Lastly, there are the C players. C players make up approximately 20 percent of your team. These employees are pulling down the organization by draining resources (getting additional training by trainers or managers), flying under the radar hoping that nobody notices, or worse yet, negatively influencing those around them. We will address this topic in more detail later in the book. For now, I want to focus on creating more As.

There are several areas requiring focus in order to create more A-level talent, either internally or from the outside. As we will be discussing recruitment techniques in later chapters, I will limit suggestions here to elevating your internal B performers to A status. Here are a few ideas:

- Take a look at the B-level talent and assess the history of each individual. Were they top performers in the past? Have they had moments of brilliance? Do they have the will to perform at a high level? With attention, do they have the potential to blossom? Are they new? Might they have been left to fend for themselves post training?
- If there is a high degree of will and the company has invested in additional training (skill), might they be better suited to alternate roles?
- Can you set up a mentoring program and align them with A players, while also allowing them to mentor others? Many times, people elevate when placed forward as performers or experts.

- Based on their will, attitude, and respect among their peers, could they be better placed in supervisory-level roles? Maybe as trainers? Often, the very best baseball/football/basketball/hockey coaches were average players; many never reached the professional level. Qualifiers for management are aptitude and attitude. While we have a tendency to promote top performers, they are often lacking in these areas. When looking for leaders, look at the role in its entirety; don't rely solely on results.

There is talent in your B performers, who play an important role in the success of the organization. Be sure to involve them, recognize them, and at all costs, avoid neglecting them. They are solid and could rise to A levels with the right commitment and attention. They could also slide to C levels without the proper amount of attention and recognition.

CHAPTER 6

FAIL FAST

Upon entering a new organization, you inherit many situations that need to be addressed. Some of the challenging situations have been created by your predecessor, while others may have come forward as a result of changes prior to your arrival. Either way, your responsibility is to correct the course. *Fail fast* relates to people, product, and process issues that need to be addressed promptly. Leadership is about listening to feedback, placing bets, taking the reins, and moving forward. I'd like to share a couple of examples—one people related and one process related. If left alone, each would have had a detrimental impact on where we wanted to take our culture.

I had just inherited a team of sales professionals who were performing at a very modest level. While there were several strong performers, they lacked the drive to compete (internally and externally) and the grit to walk through obstacles. The top performer was a consistent president's club winner. Year in and year out, he was on the trip. While he was fun and likable, he was disrespectful. From afar, I had witnessed his antics: bad-mouthing his then supervisor, talking badly about a client, talking down to his peers, and making the conscious decision that standards and rules didn't apply to him.

Prior to accepting the position, I approached my supervisor and mentioned that I would take the role on one condition—that I terminate this person, who happened to be the top rep. My supervisor was taken aback. While he knew about this rep's behaviors, he chose to look the other way. As a result, the rest of the team suffered, and leadership took a major credibility hit. As I stated earlier, if you don't stand for something, you fall for anything. This was a perfect case of that taking place in living color. I also knew that I would be judged on my action or inaction and that by allowing this level of disrespect to continue, I would be viewed in the same light as my predecessor. Finally, I knew that this team could perform better. The talent was there. The problem was that the organization had lost credibility by allowing this person to run roughshod over the values that the rest of the team lived by and stood for. I had the firm belief that this would be a perfect example of "addition by subtraction": by removing one piece, the other pieces would rise and fill the void. My supervisor agreed, and I terminated this rep on day one. Soon thereafter, my new team was recognized as the best team in the company. Fail fast when it comes to personnel issues, whether created by you (poor new hire) or someone else (poor current employee).

A second example involves a decision made to redirect all inbound client issues/complaints to a division specifically created for this purpose. Allowing a salesperson to sell something yet never requiring him or her to see the transaction through is not only poor client service but also lacks the accountability necessary to both the client and the organization. As you might imagine, as a result of this initiative, refunds rose dramatically, allowing for a choice between further burdening the client support team or dismantling this initiative and moving the responsibility of dealing with complaints back to those who should see it through. We chose the latter path. While it is certainly difficult to undo new initiatives, sometimes we just miss and need to correct the course. Do yourself a favor: set pride aside, and do what's right for your clients and your organization. Fail fast when it comes to correcting personnel decisions, changing product direction, or adjusting processes. Do nothing, and credibility falters. Do something, along with practicing full transparency throughout, and your culture thrives.

CHAPTER 7

STAY IN THE DATING STAGE

When you first inherit a new team or join a new company, it's like dating. It is fresh. It is new. It is pure bliss. Much like when you are finding a new love, you go in with the best intentions—and then reality sets in. The best relationships survive because both partners make an effort and commit to its survival.

In business, I challenge my leaders to continue to reinvent themselves. Every month/quarter, bring new elements to your approach, your calls, and your interactions. The best way to keep things fresh is by avoiding falling into a comfort zone or worse, accepting that status quo is good enough. Personal reinvention brings spice to the equation. Here are a few tactics that will work for you:

- **Get in the field, as close to every day as possible.** The action is in the field, not behind the desk. It's easy to find excuses to stay in the office, but that's not where the fun and credibility reside. Make it a point to visit every office and spend time with every employee. Let them see you in action. Break bread. Get to know your people personally. With visibility comes credibility. With credibility comes culture. Make it your goal to be active, accessible, and involved.

- **Pick up the phone and call two or three of your employees every day.** Just call to say hello and show that you care. Maybe ask for an opinion or two on something.
- **Share a laugh.** Send something funny—or better yet, self-deprecating—via e-mail to the team. Maybe lip-sync a song, shoot a funny video in the field, or do something completely unlike yourself. By putting yourself out there, you will be viewed as both approachable and relatable.
- **Schedule monthly lunches with a group of employees.** Go off-site and share some food and laughs. Keep the topic off business as much as possible. They see you enough in a business setting, through e-mails, conference calls, etc. Show the team your personal side.
- **Send cards for birthdays and anniversaries.** While a small gesture, it goes a long way to bringing the personal side into full view.
- **Send a note to the spouses/significant others of your employees, expressing thanks for allowing you to "borrow" their spouses/friends.** Maybe send fifty dollars for dinner or some flowers or candy.

Sounds like dating, doesn't it? That's because it is. The sooner you realize that your employees are being courted by others every day, the more crucial that gestures like these become. Remember, employees don't leave companies; they leave supervisors. They want to feel a connection. They want to feel valued. They want to feel alive. Keep the relationship deep and meaningful. Don't wait to do the little things. Do them now, before it's too late.

As a final piece of this chapter, I want to share why employees choose to stay at their companies. I want to be very specific here:

- Employees stay because they feel a connection to the mission.
- Employees stay because they align tightly with the corporate values.
- Employees stay because they want to be a part of something special.
- Employees stay because they feel valued.
- Employees stay because they feel that their voices matter.
- Employees stay because they are recognized.
- Employees stay because they are involved.
- Employees stay because they are proud of their organization.
- Employees stay because they see a path to advancement.
- Employees stay because they see the difference they are making within the organization.
- Employees stay because they are growing, learning, and feeling challenged.
- Employees stay because they feel a connection with their supervisors.
- Employees stay because they feel alive.
- Employees stay because they are paid well.

Take note that all but one of these listed points is intrinsic in nature and that those emotions come as a result of the corporate character and the culture that you, as a leader, have chosen to create. The key word here is *chosen*. The strength of the culture that you wish to create is completely within your control. It begins with hiring talent, identifying character, and then teaching your business. Hire will and train skill. It's all about the people. People are the engine that fuels successful organizations. With great people, great achievements are possible. Make hiring great people your absolute priority. I leave this section with a powerful quote:

> **I am convinced that nothing we do is more important than hiring and developing people. At the end of the day, you bet on people, not on strategies.**
> —Lawrence Bossidy

SECTION 2: PASSION

When you complete this section, you will be able to

1. see the need to craft and openly share your story;
2. shift from a focus on "what" to a focus on "why";
3. fully embrace the need for transparency; and
4. drive passion through aligning values and celebrating successes.

There is no passion to be found in settling for a life that is less than the one you are capable of living.

—Nelson Mandela

I n August 480 BC, a Greek force of 7,000 men, including 300 highly skilled Spartans, marched north to the narrow coastal pass of Thermopylae, also known as the Hot Gates. Their mission was to stop the aggressive advances of King Xerxes and over 150,000 Persian fighters, who were focused on expanding their empire into Ancient Greece. The Hot Gates held the only road where a sizable force could pass. The plan was for the Greek contingent to block that pass and hold off the Persian advance.

The Spartans were made up of elite fighters, born and raised to fight and defend. All men of Sparta were taken from their families at the age of seven to live in army barracks and train to become elite Spartan warriors. Their entire lives were committed to learning the art of war.

The Spartans were led by King Leonidas and for seven days, this small Greek contingent held off a much larger force. Wave after wave, the Spartans killed as many as 20,000 Persians in the Battle of Thermopylae. A local resident named Ephialtes betrayed the Greeks by revealing a mountain pass that would allow the Persians to surround the Greeks. King Leonidas dismissed the majority of his force, remaining behind with the Spartan 300, 400 Thebans, and 700 Thespian volunteers. Though they knew it meant their own deaths, they secured the escape of the other Greek forces so that they could retreat to fight another day. After seven days, King Leonidas and his men were eliminated.

According to *Merriam-Webster*, passion can be defined as "a strong feeling of enthusiasm or excitement for doing something or about doing something." The Spartan story was captured in the 2006 movie *300*. Watching the movie, reading about the Battle of Thermopylae, or studying Greek history, one cannot help but feel the emotion and passion that the Spartans had for their people and their culture and their intense commitment to protecting one another. The passion is evident in the film and in the chronicles of history.

The *why* behind the Spartan way of life was about persever-ance, preservation, and survival. Their *why* was deep and real.

This section takes us into our second P: passion. Earlier, we addressed employee brand and what to look for in current employees and future hires. Prior to identifying the team, we must first craft our *why*. In order to do this, we must ask ourselves a series of questions: Why are we in business? What do we stand for? What is our mission? What are our values? By answering these questions first, we will put ourselves in a position to clearly articulate why we do what we do. Once this is established, we can then build our story and find people who can get behind it in the same passionate way that we do. Coupling this with aligned values, we will have the makings of a passionate culture, focused forward and positively influencing the future.

CHAPTER 8

TELL YOUR STORY

I recall being excitable, full of energy, and constantly on the go when I was young. My days would consist of playing outside, literally from dawn until dusk. Then came dinner. Then came bed. And the next day, I would be back up and at it again. I recall my mom reading me books at night. As fast moving as I was during the day, I was equally slow moving in that moment. Bedtime was reading time, and reading time meant that I could be cast away and immersed in the middle of a story. As fast as my brain and body would move during the day, I was slow, deliberate, and conscious during story time.

Stories fascinate us. They resonate with us because they are authentic. They are pure. They connect us. They can become quite personal.

In 2010, photographer Brandon Stanton set out to take ten thousand photographs of people on the streets of New York and plot them on a map. Over time, Brandon started engaging with those whom he was photographing and created a blog, with short passages about each person whom he met. With this new, enhanced format, Brandon's legend began to take off. As of February 1, 2015, his book *Humans of New York* had spent twenty-nine weeks on the *New York Times* best seller list and had inspired countless additional "humans of" blogs. As of March 2016, *Humans of New York* had more than seventeen million likes on its Facebook page and three hundred thousand followers on Instagram. My children are fascinated by *Humans of New York* and read it daily. They have coffee table *Humans of New York* books, share the stories socially, and often talk about it with their friends and our family.

Storytelling and story sharing have reached a new level of interest in society. While we have always been intrigued, we are becoming a much more sensitive and outward-thinking society, so understanding people is of keen interest to us. Regardless of our ages, we are fascinated by others' plights and real-life stories.

Effective leadership calls for knowing your audience and being able to connect on a very personal level. As with the phenomenon around *Humans of New York,* your employees want to connect with you. They want to know you. They want to be able to trust you. By opening yourself up, you will be finding common ground well beyond the surface topics that we find ourselves engaged in throughout a traditional work-day. By being your authentic self, you will form a bond that will allow for your credibility and overall corporate culture to blossom.

When I move into a new role or join a new company, I make it a point to get to know every team member person-ally. I want to know what is important to him or her. I want to know what drives him or her out of bed each morning. I want to know his or her dreams and aspirations. I also want each team member to know me on a personal level. This doesn't mean that I necessarily need to be close friends. It simply means that I want the team member to know who I am and what is truly important to me. Every chance I get, I tell my story. I talk about my upbringing. I talk about my family. I talk about my personal dreams and aspirations beyond what I do during my work hours.

In addition to connecting one-on-one, I make it a point to have an "all-company" call, which all of the employees in my channel attend. This is where I tell my *why*. I talk about my family. I talk about what is important to me professionally and especially personally. I explain the reason that I chose the company. I share my personal connection with or affinity for the brand or the proposition we represent. Having grown professionally in a sales environment, I am a firm believer that people buy from people whom they like, trust, and respect. That can only occur if you let people into your world. By opening up and sharing your story, you will draw people in and connect on a much deeper and more significant level, as it is through personal connections that great cultures develop.

CHAPTER 9

FOCUS ON THE "WHY"

Years ago, leadership was easier. We motivated people with a strong compensation plan, maybe some rewards, lots of recognition, and at times fear. Today, we lead in a much more personal way. While we have always needed to understand what motivates our employees, the primary motivating factors have shifted. While money remains an important part of why people work, additional considerations have become increasingly significant. A conscious outward focus has moved the needle from "It's all about me" to "It's about me...and others."

Finding common ground with our employees has posed new opportunities for us to grow as leaders, primarily due to the size and scope of our Generation X and Generation Y workforce. Speaking personally, this workforce generation has helped me to become a more aware leader, focused outward and with others' needs more clearly in mind than ever before. My children are twenty-five and twenty-three, which classifies them as millennials, so their motivations are slightly different than mine were when I was their age. Sure, I wanted to do well by doing good, but I was much more focused inward; it was all about what I could get or what I was due. Today, that focus has shifted to what I can give, and I like it. I feel much more complete, as a person and a leader, as I have fully embraced this mind-set.

Look at the shift that has taken place in our economy over the past forty to fifty years. Between the mid-1960s and 1980, the baby boomers had roughly fifty million children. Many of these children grew up in households in which both parents worked, leaving them to fend for themselves after school. These children witnessed the commitment their parents poured into their professions while potentially sacrificing time at home with their families. In the economic downturn of the mid-1980s, many of these children watched their parents lose the jobs that they cared so much about. They grew up seeing the ugly side of business. Loyalty was no longer a cornerstone or something to value and believe in.

Then came the Generation Y (millennial) class, born between the early 1980s and the turn of the century. This group is commonly referred to as the "Trophy Kids," often recognized as receiving participation trophies for simply showing up. This generation grew up being praised and complimented in a time when "tough love" was taking a bit of a back seat. In general terms, this generation of roughly 70 million is sensitive, caring, and outwardly driven. In terms of size, Generation X and Generation Y make up approximately 36 percent of the total US population of about 325 million, and this percentage is growing daily. Depending on your line of business, that would mean that roughly one-third of your team is made up of Generation X and Generation Y employees. It would behoove all of us to understand their general wants and desires and connect with them on a mutually meaningful level.

As I mentioned earlier, there is a noticeable shift taking place in our economy, focusing outward and more deeply centered on giving than getting. Look at some of the industries and key businesses that have sprung up as a result of this shift. The obvious examples are the tech companies—Apple, Alphabet, Amazon, Twitter, Facebook, Instagram, etc. But there are also several that are not quite as obvious but still tightly entwined with the values of giving back that we've been discussing in this book so far:

- **Kiva**—Crowdfunds microloans to serve the financially excluded. Kiva created a sector of focusing outward by serving those in need.
- **The Honest Company**—A consumer goods company that emphasizes nontoxic household products to supply the market for "ethical consumerism."
- **TOMS Shoes**—In line with Kiva, this company has made a commitment to helping those in impoverished areas. Their mission is: "With every product you purchase, TOMS will help a person in need. One for one."

How can you possibly compete for outward-thinking talent when you have companies like this springing up every day? Rounding back to the title of this chapter, control what you can control and focus on your *why*.

Throughout my career, I have been involved in print advertising, digital media, recruitment, and creating marketplaces. While every venture was a for-profit initiative, each of them solved problems, alleviated pain, and created opportunity for my clients, their families, and our end users to grow, benefit, and prosper. Every business helps others. You simply need to understand and amplify your *why*. Zig Ziglar is quoted as saying, "Stop selling. Start helping." When you focus outward—on easing pain and helping others—I believe that you can compete with the big tech companies or with Kiva, the Honest Company, and TOMS. People will buy your *why* if it is stated with passion and conviction and it solves a problem or cures a pain. Take the time to clearly articulate this internally and ensure that you do the same with your team.

CHAPTER 10

MAKE TRANSPARENCY A TOP PRIORITY

I n 2014, the American Psychological Association surveyed more than 1,500 US workers and found that nearly one-quarter of them didn't trust their employers. Additionally, nearly 50 percent felt that their employers were not open and up-front with them. That, ladies and gentlemen, is an issue.

We live in a time when everything that people do is out there for public consumption. If you don't believe it, simply visit Facebook. People's lives are open and in clear view for all to see. Timely and open communication is a norm in our society today. Just watch the news. Cell phones capture the lion's share of real-time happenings in the world. So if the expectation is for timely and full disclosure in our public lives, why would it be any different in our professional lives? As leaders, why are we so guarded? According to the Dalai Lama, "A lack of transparency results in distrust and a deep sense of insecurity." I couldn't agree more.

Talking about being transparent is easy, but when it comes to actually living that standard, that's where true leadership needs to take over. In the last chapter, we spoke about why people choose to work at a particular company. We touched on the competitive landscape for talent and how you can prevail by defining your *why*. We spoke about the makeup of companies with great cultures, and the prevailing and overarching themes involved open and honest communication. We discussed what employees are looking for, and near the top of the list were feeling involved, valued, engaged, and respected. With all of this said, transparency will be critical for employee satisfaction and for building an electric and enviable culture. Without a commitment to transparency, you will be handcuffed in your quest to accomplish greatness.

I recently read a blog written by Josh James, CEO of Domo, one of the fastest-growing start-ups over the past two years. The blog addressed the idea of transparency at the board level. James felt that the Domo board should have the same level of access and transparency as the rest of the company, so he granted all board members full access to every internal Domo report. No company was granting that level of insight to its board, certainly not one with such explosive growth and scrutiny. Yet James weighed the pros and cons and moved forward. James realized that the board was in his court and that allowing this group of intelligent leaders this level of transparency would motivate his team to correct the things that weren't quite where they needed to be. Domo saw the benefits immediately. Rather than spending the week prior to a board meeting preparing decks, the company could focus on strategy and collaboration and truly tap into the brainpower amassed at the board level. Rather than talking numbers, executives could now map out further plans for growth.

The benefits of transparency are great and align tightly with the values that our employees seek:

- **Transparency promotes trust**—It states that you believe in your employees and that you are open to sharing details with them.
- **Transparency recognizes value**—It states that with more ideas and brainpower, we will further our cause.
- **Transparency flattens the organization**—With an unfiltered approach, employees have a clear line of sight into what the CEO is thinking.
- **Transparency drives "one team, one goal"**—It clearly states that we are in this together.
- **Transparency shows that you value culture**—Without openness in communication, there would be cause for potential resentment and distrust.

In order to ensure that employers practice transparency at all levels, in a unified and consistent way, I would like to share a few ideas:

1. Transparency goes both ways. Have a meeting to discuss this value. Define transparency, explain its importance, and ask for unity in execution.
2. Create a weekly/monthly newsletter that allows employees in each division to share what they are working on and what is important in their world. As the leader, share direction, results, and changes.
3. Create "task teams" to address findings from surveys and offer up solutions to improve/address. This

team will share updates on company calls and in the newsletter.

4. Work with your leadership team to ensure information cascades properly. At the close of meetings, go around the room and ensure that everyone has captured the information properly, so the team members can waterfall to their people in a consistent and meaningful way.

5. Openly admit mistakes. We all make them. Fail fast, address, and move on.

6. Address the rumor mill, whether in small groups or on a company call (planned or impromptu). Transparency calls for complete disclosure.

CHAPTER 11

OWNERSHIP THROUGH AUTHORSHIP

As leaders, we have a tendency to set our direction or set a new standard/rule, in a silo, and then share it with our teams. Rarely does the employee reaction match the visuals that we had in our minds when we developed the adjustments. The challenge is that we are in our silos, removed from the day-to-day workings of the company, and we react to what we believe our clients or employees want. By allowing our team members to shape our direction, we have a better chance at success, as they are closer to the clients, and when they have a hand in crafting a plan, they own it. This is the premise behind *ownership through authorship*.

At the center of this principle lie the corporate mission, vision, and values. I am going to suggest that this determination process extend well beyond the executive team and include a cross section of employees, organization-wide. While the company mission and vision are best set at the board and executive levels, the values will be the lifeblood of the organization and the foundation of the culture. The teams need to have a clear view into the mission and vision, so that they can travel down the path of determining the company values. Done right, the values will be the bedrock by which we define our culture, measure success, recognize performance, and determine succession planning and sustainability.

In defining corporate values, I have found that following a well-thought-out and defined process has produced the greatest outcome. I'd like to share a few learnings:

- **Start with a nomination process**—Announce that the company is looking for nominations for a team to assist in determining the company values. Explain the qualifications in full transparency (e.g., positivity, commitment, passion, etc.). Ask that people work independently and recommend people within their scope. Assess all recommendations, and choose no more than twelve. Make sure that you have representation from the majority of divisions, roles, and levels. Formally announce the committee, sharing several comments from the submitted recommendations.

- **Send a congratulations note to the chosen committee members**—Recognize them for their achievement, and set any prework expectations.

- **Set ground rules at the first meeting**—There are no bad ideas. Everyone was chosen for his or her love of the company, passion, commitment, etc. Research and bring forward general guidelines on facilitation and setting values. This will set a basic expectation for the meeting.

- **You have one vote**—Your role as leader is to facilitate. Avoid silencing debate. Guide the discussions and offer very little opinion. Play the scribe role, or nominate someone else, and sit back and watch.

- **Share the values in place at present**—Debate their merits, and open the topic for discussion.

- **Limit the group to a maximum of twelve members**—Optimally, settle on six or seven. With more than twelve, full involvement and consensus will be difficult.

- **Ensure that the values are authentic and specific**—Use easy phrases; avoid complexity or ambiguity.

- **Share the output with the senior leadership team**—This is more about ensuring alignment than making adjustments. If values are askew, that's on you as the leader and facilitator. If you need to make adjustments, call the committee back together to discuss them. The committee needs to be the ultimate approving party.

- **Share company-wide**—This is a big deal and needs to be done in a full company meeting and in the form of a celebration. No other messaging should accompany this communication. It is exclusively meant to share values.

- **Have the committee share the values**—This process is about inclusion and ownership. If you roll it out, it won't have the same impact as it will if the committee members do it.

- **Recognize the committee publicly**—After the committee rolls out the values, share your thoughts and speak about the process and the people involved. Your support will matter to the process and to those involved.

- **Implement a monthly/quarterly award**—The award should align directly with each of the core values. Implement a written nomination process, and have the executive team vote on winners each month or quarter. Announce recipients at monthly/quarterly recognition meetings. Pass out small trophies/plaques and gift cards. The trophies will serve to remind the person, and anyone who comes by his or her desk, of the significance placed on the organizational values.
- **Make this your introductory presentation for new hires**—This will emphasize the significance placed on organizational values and help confirm to new hires that they have joined an organization that aligns well with their personal values.
- **Frame copies of the values and distribute one to every office**—These should be placed in a prominent area for all to see.

Remember, if it's important to you, it will be important to all. The team will flex as you flex. If you embody the values and speak to them through words, actions, and recognition, they will become the foundation of your culture and attract talent from far and wide.

CHAPTER 12

CELEBRATE EVERYTHING

Nothing influences behavior, good or not so good, quite like immediate recognition. My wife, Diane, and I have a six-month-old goldendoodle named Winston. Diane is training Winston to hopefully become a comfort dog, visiting sick children and senior citizens. Talk about an outward-focused human—that's my wife. Raising a comfort dog takes years of training and discipline, with a very low percentage of dogs actually graduating to become a certified comfort dog. We have hired a trainer (who's wonderful, by the way), and she has taught us much about training but more importantly, she has taught us about ourselves. She shared that I am not a pack leader (imagine that!) and that I need to become one. So I can't sit on the ground, look Winston in the eyes, or even pay attention to him. What's the fun in having a dog if I can't pal around with him?

The point of the trainer's message is about immediately recognizing the behavior we want (giving Winston a treat when he does well to reinforce the behavior) and avoiding recognizing behavior we don't want (pulling when we walk him, barking, etc.). The outcome is that when we recognize the good behavior, he will want to do more of that, because treats follow. This leads us to this chapter and the need to *celebrate everything*.

Recognition is a powerful tool to drive culture and reinforce the behaviors we seek. It comes in many shapes and sizes. It doesn't have to be expensive. Often, the recognition is nothing more than an unexpected call or a random e-mail. The point is that it takes a conscious effort to create a recognition-rich culture. When you couple great people with consistent and genuine recognition, you have the makings of a passion-filled environment.

There are countless benefits to embracing a recognition-rich culture:

- **Recognition aligns with personal needs**—On a primal level, everyone has a need for recognition and praise.
- **Recognition drives productivity**—Much like Winston, when someone feels good, he or she longs to get more of that feeling: more success, more recognition.
- **Recognition influences profitability**—Studies conducted by Disney and Sears illustrate a direct correlation between improved staff satisfaction scores and directly recognizable increases in revenue.
- **Recognition makes B players into A players**—Recognition is not limited to top performers. As mentioned in the first bullet, praise is a primal need. If a person is told that he or she is good, he or she will learn to believe it and seek more recognition of it.
- **Recognition will create internal sponsors**—Word will get out quickly, and those recognized will be cheerleaders for the organization.

- **Recognition will create external sponsors**—Great people know great people, and they won't hesitate to share their passion for their organization and to recommend to their friends that they join.
- **Recognition will reduce churn**—Successful people will have no need to look elsewhere when their needs are being met by your organization.

Recognition comes in many varieties. I classify them as daily, weekly, monthly, quarterly, and annual:

- **Daily**—The best way to influence today's behavior is by recognizing yesterday's achievements. When you arrive at work in the morning, take a look at your previous day's performance. Take note of the top one or two performers, as well as a couple of people who performed well in subjective areas (good client feedback, peer recognition, etc.). Ask your leaders to send you a note whenever a person does something great, and call that person to thank him or her. Make this part of your daily "grateful" outreach.
- **Weekly**—If you perform a weekly stack rank, share that internally, recognizing those who lead the pack or those who are trending well. Also, if you are in a monthly/quarterly business where pace plays a role, be sure to recognize those who are setting the tone, ahead of pace.
- **Monthly**—Get in the habit of doing monthly all-company recognition calls in which the emphasis is on recognizing the top performers by channel for the previous month. During this call, be sure to read out

client testimonials received in the prior month. If you had an incentive in place, be sure to share winners at this time as well.

- **Quarterly**—Again, implement recognition calls, if you don't do them monthly. Prepare a deck, complete with pictures, accomplishments, stories, etc.

- **Annual**—If you work in an incentive-laden environment (sales), introduce an annual achiever's club to recognize annual achievement with a trip, gala, etc. Share updates weekly, monthly, and quarterly. Be sure to include support and other divisions as well. Maybe send an update to the employee's spouse or friend, sharing the progress that the employee is achieving.

When an executive takes the time to recognize superior achievement, the benefits are potentially game changing. That level of motivational currency is worth its weight in gold. If you do this consistently, you will create a recognition-rich culture that will permeate your entire organization. This takes effort, and it takes commitment. There are very few levers that can elicit the level of enhanced productivity that recognition can deliver. Commit to celebrating success and forward movement.

SECTION 3: PROPOSITION

When you complete this section, you will be able to

1. determine if there is a need and if not, what to do about it;
2. internalize your proposition; and
3. be focused on your elevator pitch, your USP, and your value proposition.

If everyone else is doing it one way, you can find your niche by going in exactly the opposite direction.

—Sam Walton

I n his book *Start with Why*, Simon Sinek states the following:

There's barely a product or service on the market today that customers can't buy from someone else for about the same price, about the same quality, about the same level of service, and about the same features. If you truly have a first-mover's advantage, it's probably lost in the first few months. If you offer something truly novel, someone else will soon come up with something similar or maybe even better.

Sinek developed a principle called the golden circle, which challenges leaders to think from the inside out. Here is an illustration of the principle:

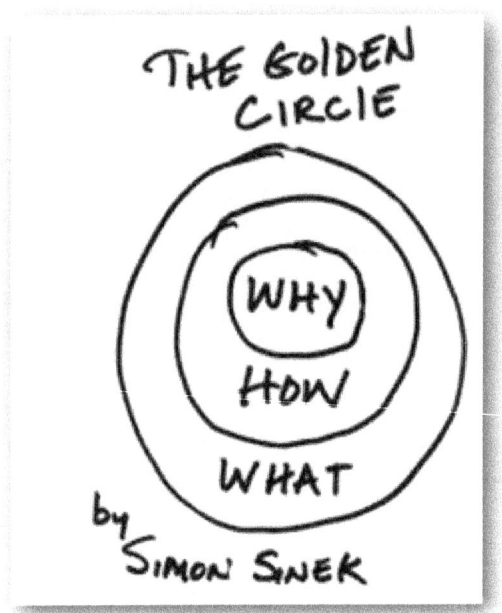

1. **What**—Every company in the world can explain what it does. These are the products it sells or the services it offers.

2. **How**—Some companies know what they do and how they do it. "Hows" are normally identified by how a company's proposition is different from others (unique selling proposition - USP).

3. **Why**—Very few organizations know why they do what they do. "Why" is not about making money. That is the result. "Why" is about purpose, belief, cause, and passion. It is the very reason the company exists.

When employees or organizations communicate their stories, they usually do so from the outside in, explaining what they do, maybe how they do it, and rarely why they do what they do. The truly great companies start with *why*, as they understand that people buy based on an emotional connection to a product, service, or company.

Sinek shares a story about Apple. He articulates the company's process of leading with "why," moving to "how," and ending at "what":

Everything we do, we believe in challenging the status quo. We believe in thinking differently...The way we challenge the status quo is by making our products beautifully designed, simple to use, and user friendly. And we happen to make great computers.

When an organization articulates its "why," we feel a more personal connection, and as a result, we go out of our way to be associated with that brand and to bring it openly into our lives. We embrace its beliefs, as they align with our values and beliefs. The organization and the brand touch an emotional part of our brain, and we feel a personal connection.

When we look to develop allegiance among our employees and clients, we must start with "why," engaging emotionally. In the end, people don't buy *what* you do; they buy *why* you do it.

CHAPTER 13

IS THERE A NEED?

To improve is to change; to be perfect is to change often.

—Winston Churchill

I love this quote, as it captures the essence of business beautifully.

A critically important part of ensuring that you develop a healthy culture and a thriving business involves the evolution of your product, service, or proposition. A leader's responsibility is to know when to maintain, when to change, and how much to change, while consistently keeping an eye on the future.

In order to understand if there is a need, do your research to determine the market potential, sizing up which players own what share of the market and studying your trajectory. Get your hands on as much market intelligence on your competitors as possible (pricing, target demographic, marketing approach, etc.). Study your unique selling proposition. If your business is growing, avoid sitting back. If you're not moving forward, you're moving backward. Success is an evolution and takes forward thinking and an on-your-toes mentality. If you sit still and get comfortable, others will pass you buy. Consider these examples:

- *Encyclopedia Britannica* was a staple in nearly every household and every library for 244 years. It was *the* tool, used by students far and wide in the pre-Internet age. In March 2012, overtaken by the likes of Wikipedia and Google, *Encyclopedia Britannica* published its last edition. What could have been done? What should have been done?
- **R. H. Donnelley** published the first yellow pages back in 1886. At one time, R. H. Donnelley was a behemoth, widely respected as the premier advertising vehicle for small businesses. Businesses needed the yellow pages to compete and thrive. Today, print media is a dying industry, and R. H. Donnelley, operating under the name Dex, is a mere shell of its once-proud days, attempting to morph to digital but facing steep competition. Should R. H. Donnelley have anticipated the move to digital advertising sooner? Could it have avoided its current state with a long-term strategy?

There are countless stories in which companies missed the wave and got caught in the riptide. As leaders, we have a responsibility to our people, our clients, and our shareholders to reinvent and to discover. Curiosity is a key attribute of the most effective leaders.

On the other side of the equation, I offer examples in which companies made the pivot successfully and now find themselves with household-name status. They broke through when their chances were seemingly slim at the onset:

- **Starbucks**—It opened in Seattle in 1971 as an operation selling coffee beans and espresso machines. In the early 1980s, Howard Schultz (current CEO) joined as the director of retail operations. Howard attempted to convince the then owners to go one step further and make and sell drinks. The owners refused, and Howard left to open a shop called Il Giornale. Howard eventually purchased Starbucks, renamed his store, and was off to the races. He likely would have made a nice living working for the previous owners of Starbucks, but he had different plans. He had the vision to see the future and the fortitude to see it through.

- **Groupon**—In 2007, Andrew Mason launched the Point, which was based on a tipping point principle, wherein people would donate to a cause, but the cause would only receive the funds if the fund-raising goal was achieved, thus tripping the tipping point. In 2008, with the help of Eric Lefkofsky, the Point made a pivot to focus on the retail benefits of group purchasing, utilizing the same tipping point principle and Groupon (Group Coupon) was born. The Point likely would have never hit anyone's radar. Today, Groupon is a household name.

- **Twitter**—Previously named Odeo, Twitter began as a podcast subscription service but quickly realized that iTunes was cornering the market on podcasts. Within two weeks, Odeo rebranded as Twitter and pivoted to an idea of becoming a status update blogging platform, conceived by Jack Dorsey and Biz Stone. Today, Twitter has more than nine hundred million accounts and more than three hundred million active users. Twitter made a bold pivot, and it paid off.

- **Instagram**—Began as a gaming and photo app called BURBN. It morphed and became too similar to Foursquare, so BURBN pivoted to focusing exclusively on photography. I'd say it was a good move.
- **Pinterest**—Begun as an iPhone app called Tote, Pinterest was basically a megacatalogue for shoppers on the go, set to share updates when certain items went on sale. The company found that most people engaged with the site by putting together collections and sharing those ideas with friends. Pinterest saw the market, watched how its users interacted with the site, and adjusted to meet the needs of its users. Today, Pinterest has seventy million users.

These five stories are great examples of companies that understood the market and the needs of users and had the foresight and conviction to move ahead in a different direction. I'd like to close this chapter with a quote from all-time great Wayne Gretzky: "I skate to where the puck is going to be, not to where it has been." Learn from the past, study, anticipate, head up, and look ahead.

CHAPTER 14

WHAT IS YOUR USP?

In determining the path you wish to travel, you must first identify how you will be defined as unique by those who have choices about who to do business with. Nearly every business has a competitor, someone to whom it may often be compared. The key is to find your spot and to craft a message (your proposition) so that you stand unique in what may be a crowded field vying for mindshare. Your ability to create uniqueness will be paramount to your avoiding commoditization. One way to know that you've missed the mark is having people ask for the price. This is a pretty clear indication that they have a comparison in mind. To avoid price considerations and being viewed as a commodity, identify your unique selling proposition (USP).

In order to set yourself apart, begin with the outcome in mind. In other words, it's not about what you are selling but rather what problem you will solve for your user. As an example, consider Dollar Shave Club. In 2012, Michael Dubin decided that there was a better way for men to buy razor blades. Think about the industry. Over the decades, there has been very little (if any) innovation beyond adding blades, pivots, and gel strips. Michael took a look at the challenges and saw potential to adjust the outcome in his favor. He saw blades as a necessary evil—something that everyone needed. He saw two challenges: they were terribly overpriced, and you actually had to go to the store and buy them. He zeroed in on two areas—cost and convenience. He came up with a fun and witty advertising campaign that went viral, and his business took off. Dollar Shave Club currently has more than one million subscribers and a valuation in excess of $600 million for a product that has lacked true innovation since its invention in 1901. He identified the issue, worked to solve the problem, and completely disrupted a multibillion-dollar industry.

In determining your USP, I'd like to offer the following thoughts for your consideration:

- **Focus on the result you will provide, not what you are selling**—In the end, people will buy the "why," not the "what." Focus on solving problems rather than on the product or service you are selling.
- **Make an emotional connection**—Go out of your way to find commonality and an emotional connection point. Deliver on your promises with a compulsiveness to delight. Make a commitment to overdelivering on expectations.
- **Overemphasize your uniqueness to sidestep comparisons**—Much the same way Dollar Shave Club developed a brand for cool and committed to cost and convenience, find your uniqueness and drive it hard.
- **It's not about price**—Sure, your pricing strategy is critical, but in most cases, it is not why people buy.

People buy because you uniquely solve a problem for them. People will never question price if their pain is real, you can solve it, and you care every step along the way.

- **Know your audience and appeal to them, even at the expense of other segments**—Look at Abercrombie & Fitch. The company is not looking for a fifty-five-year-old male customer, and it overtly makes that point. Abercrombie & Fitch is focused on a completely different demographic and makes no bones about it.

CHAPTER 15

INTERNALIZE INTERNALLY

Once you've settled on your USP, it is time for your entire company to internalize it. How clearly can you articulate your USP? Before you can take it to the team, it must be perfected and internalized by the leadership team. This is a necessary step in creating consistent messaging and a passionate environment. After all, this is your brand. Articulating a well-thought-out and measured message, practiced by all, is the first step in defining your brand outwardly.

There are three components to internalizing your proposition: the elevator pitch, the USP, and the value prop. Each is used differently and in different settings. Let's get deeper into each of them:

- **Elevator pitch**—An elevator pitch is intended to be succinct and persuasive while *not* being viewed as a sales pitch. It is informal, casual, and a comfortable way to share the benefit of your offering without sounding "salesy" or robotic. This would be a good spot to incorporate your *why*. There are three components to the elevator pitch: benefit statement, differentiator, and next step.

o **Benefit statement**—It is the outcome of using your product or service. For example: "Companies use us to get their message in front of new homeowners within forty-eight hours of their arrival at their new homes, enhancing their opportunity to secure a long-term relationship with their brand." In leading with *why*, the benefit statement might look something like this: "Moving homes is very difficult on children and families. We are committed to making the process easier by helping families feel comfortable in acclimating to their new surroundings."

o **Differentiator**—This is where you stand out as being unique in the way that you bring your product or service forward. For example: "We do this by partnering with the US Postal Service, printing the new mover welcome kits, which ensures credibility, accuracy, timeliness, and consistency."

o **Next step**—This is *not* a close; it is simply a request to discuss your pitch in more detail at a later time. It is very nonthreatening and meant to be respectful of the current surroundings while ensuring that there is a go-forward step. For example: "It would be great if we could get some time to discuss this further. What does your schedule look like in the next couple of weeks?"

The elevator pitch is an important step in creating interest in a precise yet casual way. You need to really practice here, so as to avoid an unnatural feel and maintain a casual flow. It needs to be done in a "real" voice, person to person, and not come off as an infomercial. It needs to be about the *why* and not the *what* and to have a clear "I want to help" feel to it. Once you master it, every single person on your staff needs to master it as well. Every person on your staff knows people, and we are all responsible for moving our respective organizations forward. You never know when one of your employees will play a critical role in securing a relationship for your firm. Train everyone in the elevator pitch.

- **The unique selling proposition**—Discussed in the last chapter, the USP is what sets you apart from others within your space. Your USP needs to be specific and unique to your offering. Critical at the decision point, the USP could mean the difference between being viewed as a commodity, with price sensitivity attached, and having a truly unique offering that will address the pain that the customer is experiencing.

- **The value proposition**—People won't buy from you if they don't have any reason to pay attention to you. Your value proposition describes the value that you will bring to the end user. It's the main reason that a person will buy from you over your competitors. If available, your value proposition should include statistics and testimonials: these can have a profound impact. Your value proposition should be the first thing listed on your website. In most highly competitive industries, you will see testimonials and statistics right on the home page.

I worked with a CEO who started out in the food service industry, where he was exposed to the saying: "Burger on the bun, cheese on the burger, pickle on the cheese." This phrase resonated with me, as it was all about consistency and predictability. I saw this as a mantra for sales as well. Whether a salesperson was speaking to a client in Miami or Spokane, those customers would be greeted in the same way and hear the story (elevator pitch, USP, and value proposition) in the exact same way. That level of consistency will dictate your brand. I know that if I walk into a McDonald's anywhere in the world, my burger is going to taste exactly the same. That is because McDonald's leaves nothing to chance when it comes to quality, consistency, and its brand. Ensure that you put the same effort toward your brand: burger on the bun, cheese on the burger, pickle on the cheese.

SECTION 4: PROCESS

When you complete this section, you will be able to

1. understand the significance of creating and following a repeatable and predictable process;
2. have a clear understanding of the tools available to you; and
3. realize the importance of consistency in every aspect of your business.

Start-up success is not a consequence of good genes or being in the right place at the right time. Success can be engineered by following the right process, which means it can be learned, which means it can be taught.

—Eric Ries

In 1995, Jack Welch, while serving as CEO of General Electric, made the process of Six Sigma central to his overall organizational strategy. Six Sigma is a disciplined, data-driven approach and methodology for eliminating defects (driving toward six standard deviations between the mean and the nearest specification limit) in any process—from manufacturing to transactional and from product to service. In other words, it is a set of techniques and tools to improve your process and results.

Six Sigma has a specific set of goals. Reducing costs, increasing profits, and driving customer satisfaction are examples of Six Sigma targets. There is a clear focus on data-driven decisions, rather than assumptions and gut feelings. Every Six Sigma initiative involves a keen focus on achieving quantifiable and measured results.

There is a specific protocol utilized when making changes to an existing process and a separate protocol used when implementing a new process:

- DMAIC—Used when making improvements to an existing process. The acronym stands for define, measure, analyze, improve, and control.
- DMADV—Used when developing new processes. The acronym stands for define, measure, analyze, design, and verify.

There is a certification process to become a green or black belt in Six Sigma.

Please understand that I am not certified as a Six Sigma expert, nor am I recommending that you be certified unless you choose to head down that path. While a highly worthwhile and tremendously beneficial process, it is a commitment, and it is formal and regimented. The reason I want to share Six Sigma is to help you understand the need for process within business. Thousands of companies have implemented Six Sigma to great success. Having a well-understood and fully embraced process, whether it is as formal as Six Sigma or not, is a necessity in business. I am a staunch believer that having a solid process in place will lead to consistent and predictable results in your business. In this section, we will be reviewing a series of techniques and tools that will bring consistency to your approach and predictability to your outcome.

Often, process can be misconstrued as micromanagement, as it involves setting guidelines and expectations as well as measurement and accountability. That said, without a disciplined and consistent way of doing things, the result will be inconsistency and unpredictability. This section will assist you in looking at each element of your business and ensuring that there are well-thought-out steps to each of them. Whether developing training, recruiting talent, or mapping compensation, having a clear and understood process is a critical need in business.

CHAPTER 16

IDENTIFY YOUR KPIS

Think of yourself as a pilot. Imagine having to fly a plane blindly, with no line of sight, no altimeter, no airspeed indicator, and no compass. Your chances of landing that plane would rely solely on your judgment, your intuition, and your reactions. Given the choice, you would most certainly request gauges, as gauges allow you to have confidence in your direction.

Think of key performance indicators (KPIs) as your business instrument panel. With strong and well-thought-out KPIs, you greatly enhance your ability to find success and land your plane. Without them, you would be relying solely on judgment, which would make a successful outcome significantly more difficult.

The first step in developing an effective set of KPIs is to determine the organization's strategic vision. A strategic vision is basically a view into what you want to create in the future. Being able to articulate this is the first step in being able to make that vision a reality. Once you've created your strategic vision, it's time to determine the sequence of steps and the benchmarks to achieve the vision.

As in any goal-setting exercise, we begin building our KPIs with the acronym SMART in mind:

- **S**—*Specific*—Detail the opportunity ahead. Is the goal clear and unambiguous?
- **M**—*Measurable*—We must build quantitative or qualitative metrics by which to measure progress.
- **A**—*Attainable*—Can we deploy resources to the opportunity to influence the outcome? Do we agree that this opportunity is achievable?
- **R**—*Relevant*—Does our goal matter? Is it aligned with the overall goals of the organization?
- **T**—*Time-bound*—A commitment to a deadline keeps the team focused on benchmarking to a successful outcome.

There are three levels of KPIs that must be developed:

1. **Business KPIs**—These KPIs are broad in nature and easily relatable to all employees. These will be at the center of every all-team meeting and newsletter. They will serve as the cornerstone of success for the organization and will be fully transparent.
2. **Department KPIs**—Every department should have a set of departmental KPIs that they share internally and with the executive team weekly. Business heads should be responsible for developing and compiling weekly KPI progress reports and sharing those results with their team members as well as other department

heads on the executive team. These goals will be specific to the respective departments and align upward with the overall organizational goals and business KPIs.

3. **Individual KPIs**—Sometimes referred to as individual metrics, these are the levers that influence individual outcomes. As an example, the overall sales organization has a monthly revenue goal that is shared as a full business KPI. Each individual within the organization has an individual goal for each month, which rolls up to the departmental and organizational goal. In order to achieve the individual goal, each salesperson will have a daily activity expectation that, when coupled with a conversion goal, will lead to his or her monthly achievement. The daily activity goals (meetings or quality conversations) and the daily conversion rate would effectively serve as individual KPIs. Said another way, they are the activities that lead to the overall goal.

The last set of definitions are important to understand, in order to know where to look and what to view to determine progress or regression:

1. **Quantitative measures**—This is the most common type of KPI, as it is specific to numbers. Sales, call volumes, net margin, and conversion rates are all quantitative measures.

2. **Qualitative measures**—These are more subjective in nature and open to interpretation. They may involve differentiating and determining results around

varied classes of data, interpretation of survey results, or discussion of trend lines.

3. **Leading indicators**—Early predictors of sales, revenue, or profit. As an example, if an organization notes an increasing trend in client dissatisfaction, this would be a leading indicator that there could be a risk to the annual budget projections. On the other hand, early adoption and strong client feedback on a new product launch would be significant leading indicators for success in a given quarter. Leading indicators are hard to interpret yet easier to influence.

4. **Lagging indicators**—Are typically output oriented. They are easy to interpret but impossible to influence in the measurement period.

5. **Benchmarking**—These are the pieces that make up the whole. This is an important part of the process of determining if the organization is on pace to achieve its goals. Benchmarking allows you to adjust your plan should you find your team falling behind.

In determining strategic KPIs, most organizations are intently focused on several key areas of their business—financial, sales and marketing, client, and employee. Here are several relatively standard KPIs by key area:

- **Financial**—Net profit, net profit margin, gross profit margin, EBITDA, revenue growth rate.
- **Sales and marketing**—Annual client spend, number of new clients, average deal size, LTV, net revenue, year-over-year traffic, year-over-year lead flow, conversion rate.
- **Client**—Client retention rate, net promoter score.

- **Employee**—Employee satisfaction, average tenure, employee churn, churn reasons, 360 feedback.

Now that we have the definitions out of the way, where does that leave us? This is where definition meets action and alignment drives productivity:

- **Define and agree**—You must first go off-site, free of distractions, and lock down with your executive team. The board and CEO have mapped the strategic vision, and it's time to map out and drive KPIs. This is a stake-in-the-ground moment, when each executive brings forward his or her commitments that align with his or her respective KPIs. Don't leave that meeting until everyone has aligned to the corporate imperatives and committed to KPIs that will lead to team and organizational success.
- **Build a compensation plan**—As much as we'd like to believe that people will do what's right for the business, at the end of the day, they will do what you pay them to do. If you are serious about driving culture, aligning all players, and ultimately achieving goals, you must build a compensation plan that drives the activities that lead to the outcome. Again, you will get what you are willing to pay for.
- **Communicate**—Set up a full company call in which the CEO shares the strategic vision. Each executive then shares his or her individual division commitments to the company. Each month (in a newsletter or on a call), each executive restates his or her KPIs and shares progress toward those goals.

- **Invest in visual tools**—Graphs over numbers and pictures over words. Data visualization tools are an important part of studying progress and success, and they are easy to share with others. Bring light to the darkness.

- **Have a steady hand**—Resist the urge to adjust at the first sign of stumble. The easiest thing to do is to adjust goals. The hardest thing to do is to be steadfast in your resolve. Place yourself back in the executive session where the goals and KPIs were developed. By using the SMART method, you all agreed that the goals were attainable. Unless some new advancement or competitive threat has completely altered your ability to succeed, you must do the heavy lifting and build plans to achieve the set and agreed-to goals. Success is never a straight line but is rather full of left turns, right turns, peaks, and valleys.

- **Weekly executive KPI meetings**—This is when each executive comes prepared to discuss his or her KPI progress. Designate someone from the business intelligence/analytics team to organize the pre-work, facilitate the weekly session, and review the dashboards. Done right, this is a one-hour session. As challenges unfold, new plans are developed. The goal is to address, correct the course, and monitor progress over the next week. By committing to a weekly accountability session, you can pivot much more quickly, allowing for a more timely and more substantive impact. Do not reschedule these meetings. Make them a priority.

- **Recognize and celebrate**—Share openly and often, especially at the executive level. Recognize progress, celebrating the advancements made by each department head. This is really important, as reinforcement will not only advance the cause but also form bonds at the leadership level. Monthly, be sure to share the successes outward beyond the executive team, again recognizing the successes, challenges, and opportunities.

In *Lead from the Front*, I state, "You can't manage what you can't measure." It is imperative that KPIs become part of your corporate DNA. In a metrics-driven company in which accountability is front and center, results are certain to follow. Success comes from actions, and actions come from a purposeful vision and a commitment to KPIs at all levels and by all employees.

CHAPTER 17

BUILD YOUR PLAN

I n Stephen Covey's book *First Things First*, he shares a story that consistently resonates with me and is important as we kick off this chapter.

In the middle of a seminar on time management, Covey recalls the lecturer saying, "OK, it's time for a quiz." Reaching under the table, he pulled out a wide-mouthed gallon jar and set it on the table next to a platter covered with fist-size rocks. "How many of these rocks do you think we can get in the jar?" he asked the audience. After the students made their guesses, the seminar leader said, "OK, let's find out." He put one rock in the jar, then another, then another, until no more rocks would fit. Then he asked, "Is the jar full?" Everybody could see that not one more of the rocks would fit, so they said, "Yes."

"Not so fast," the lecturer cautioned. From under the table, he lifted out a bucket of gravel, dumped it in the jar, and shook it. The gravel slid into all the little spaces left by the big rocks. Grinning, the seminar leader asked once more, "Is the jar full?"

A little wiser by now, the students responded, "Probably not."

"Good," the teacher said. Then he reached under the table to bring up a bucket of sand. He started dumping the sand in the jar. While the students watched, the sand filled in the little spaces left by the rocks and gravel. Once more, he looked at the class and asked, "Now, is the jar full?"

"No," everyone shouted back.

"Good!" said the seminar leader, who then grabbed a pitcher of water and began to pour it into the jar. He got something like a quart of water into that jar before he said, "Ladies and gentlemen, the jar is now full. Can anybody tell me the lesson you can learn from this? What's my point?"

An eager participant spoke up: "Well, there are gaps in your schedule. And if you really work at it, you can always fit more into your life."

"No," the leader said. "That's not the point. The point is this: if I hadn't put those big rocks in first, I would never have gotten them in."

In both our business and personal lives, we have big rocks, gravel, sand, and water. The natural tendency seems to favor the latter three elements, leaving little space for the big rocks. In an effort to respond to the urgent, we sometimes set aside the important.

In this chapter, we are going to discuss how we go about identifying our priorities and how to address them. Your plan should look out thirty, sixty, and ninety days. There are two main reasons that you build a specific plan. The first is to win the trust of your people, allowing them to feel involved, to feel that you care, and to know that you are all on the same page and moving in the same direction. It is critical that those most affected by change have a direct voice in influencing it. Allowing people to help shape the future leads to building great cultures and affords your employees the things that they seek most: intrinsic value, a feeling of worth, and a sense of belonging to something greater than themselves.

The second reason that you build a thirty-sixty-ninety-day plan is often overlooked yet incredibly important. It is to ensure the support of your peers and your supervisor. To embark on a plan solo, without the full buy-in of your supervisor, is a surefire way to create distance, alienation, and poor support. You cannot identify and address issues without your boss having your back. In many instances, your boss may have had a hand in authoring many of the challenges that exist today. To undo those initiatives would mean that your boss would have to admit poor judgment or a bad decision. Great leaders can accept that. Many leaders cannot. Ensure that you have the backing to address challenges and opportunities and a fully supportive green light to move forward. This will also create your scorecard for success, which will be important when it comes time to assess your worth and potential path to promotion.

Let's begin by addressing how you uncover the key components that will make up the foundation of your plan:

- **Survey your employees**—As discussed previously, kick off your new role or the new year with a survey. This will form the basis for determining your priorities and, ultimately, your big rocks. Be sure to qualitatively and quantitatively dissect the findings. Print out all pages of the survey and place them into a binder by role type. Read everything several times. Highlight consistent areas of opportunity, and begin to prioritize based on the number of common themes and the strength of the opinions expressed.

- **Meet with members of the executive team**—This will give you perspective on how the team views the current landscape and ideas the team has about challenges and opportunities on the horizon. Dig deep. Their perceptions matter and will offer a bit of a credible outsider's view. Share preliminary findings from the employee survey and gauge the executive team's initial thoughts and level of support.
- **Meet with your peers or other executives**—Once surveys have been completed and specific ideas formulated, bounce them off your leadership team as part of a sanity check. Let the team help shape the priorities.
- **Meet with several of the top performers who report up through your channel**—This is an additional level of confirmation from a group that is critically important to win over, allowing them to feel a part of the decision-making team.

Once you have the survey findings compiled and have met with each of the respective groups outlined above, you will begin to build out your plan:

- **Thirty-day plan**—*Get them thinking.* In this stage, on day one, you commit to a process and start to openly communicate what the team can expect as a result of its input and involvement. Schedule an all-company call within your first few days. Share your beliefs, your passion, and your values. Let people get to know you personally. Let them know that your passion and motivation lie with seeing them succeed. Share your plan about surveying and what the team can expect thereafter. Remember, having a new leader can be intimidating. The sooner that you can ease that tension, the better. The more that you show your openness and approachability, the more the team will support you and rally around the cause. When mapping out your first thirty days, rather than incorporating goals such as "meet with people," be very thoughtful on the exact people with whom you will meet, as well as specific days and times. It is important that you live the roles that you are surveying, so you can understand the perspectives of the employees in each role. The first thirty days require immersion. In order to determine the scope of change and prioritize appropriately, you must live the role. Through your survey and your immersion, you will get a clear view into the areas requiring the most immediate attention. Some of those may very well be the biggest of your rocks. While I would shy away from tackling the biggest rocks within the first thirty days, there are times when issues are too clear to avoid and therefore must be addressed promptly. Tackle them decisively. Again, your first thirty days involve immersion, asking, learning, and seeking advice and counsel. Take notes and form opinions. Start shaping your plan and taking action.

Your first thirty days will form the first impression that the team will have of you. Be viewed as the person who walks the talk and is committed to the cause and to listening to the needs of the people. Within the first thirty days, bring your direct reports together. Prepare a full deck, complete with survey findings, big rocks, strategy, timing, standards, and expectations. Have the full executive leadership team in attendance as a show of unity and a commitment to the go-forward strategy. In the first thirty days, make your way around and meet as many people as possible. Commit to observation. Start assessing your talent and determining those who will be part of the solution going forward. Assess your recruitment needs (additional and replacement), and begin to map a plan of attack. Change the comp plan. Illustrate to the team that you are willing to give to get (we will discuss this in greater detail shortly). Perform a SWOT analysis (strengths, weaknesses, opportunities, threats) and set SMART goals.

- **Sixty-day plan**—*Get them doing.* In month two, it is time to implement plans and set standards around expectations. Take action on needs as a result of the survey and development of the big rocks. Open and transparent communication is imperative during this stage, as it is important that the team view your ability to follow through on survey commitments. Goals have been clearly articulated, and KPIs and success measures are in place and openly being shared. The tone is set for celebrating successes. It is also time to start addressing talent deficiencies. You will need to work closely with HR to ensure alignment on building the go-forward plan and team. Be visible. During times of change, it is important to be front and center. Be an accessible leader, the champion for positivity in change. Invest in training and development at both the individual and leadership levels.

- **Ninety-day plan**—*Get them passionate.* Openly share changes and the early results of these changes. Have confidence in the plan, and embrace and recognize those who are living the values and elevating their performances. Where the first thirty days constituted a feeling-out period, month three is when leaders emerge, and those who will be part of the future plan begin to elevate their performance and embrace the full vision of the organization. Recognition and confirmation are important during this stage, as there will likely be personnel adjustments in month three. The big rocks are now in place and being executed upon. Reviewing data and tweaking direction are important in this stage. Let the numbers, rather than intuition, dictate direction. Follow what the data is telling you.

The keys to building an effective ninety-day plan are open communication and buy-in from the executive team. Most leaders fail when they don't anchor or commit to a strategy and when they hesitate in their execution. Build a plan that is strategically sound, and execute it with confidence and unwavering conviction. Be slow and thoughtful in assessing and decisive in execution. Be conscious of the effects of change, both positive and negative. Relate to how people may be feeling by being open with your thoughts and compassionate in your communications. The ninety-day plan sets the tone for the direction of the organization and the culture that will ensue. Err on the side of being aggressive and dreaming big. Your performers will thank you, and your organization will benefit as a result.

CHAPTER 18

RECRUITMENT

Success in business is all about people, people, people. Whatever industry a company is in, its employees are its biggest competitive advantage.

—Sir Richard Branson

There is a war for talent, and it will continue for as long as anyone reading this book is alive. There will be ebbs and flows in our economy, which will have an impact on our current employee retention; however, the fact remains that we have a shrinking workforce, and talent will always be in demand. The leverage will be with the employee from this point forward. The sooner that every leader realizes this fact, the better he or she will be able to address it and work through it. Here are a couple of eye-opening stats:

- According to Pew Research, the majority of the US workforce are currently in their twenties (53.5 million millennials, 52.7 million Generation Xers, 44.6 million baby boomers).

- According to the report "America's Aging Workforce Crisis," workers under the age of thirty-five spend an average of twenty months on the job, and 70 percent of college grads will leave their first postgraduation job within two years.
- According to the Bureau of Labor Statistics, on average, ten thousand baby boomers (those born between 1946 and 1964) retire every day.

In this chapter, we will take a look at the recruitment process to ensure that we are prepared to win in the war for talent. First, a few callouts and reminders:

- **Connect**—As stated in the "America's Aging Workforce Crisis" report, by the year 2020, Generation Y will make up 43 percent of the American workforce. Earlier in the book, we covered what employees want in a career. Most notably, they want meaningful work within a meaningful culture. We must connect on a highly visceral level. In order to attract and keep talent, this must be our absolute top priority, or we will lose people as quickly as we gain them, keeping us from growing and advancing our organization. Those organizations that focus on cause and culture will flourish as the workforce dynamic shifts.
- **Put employees first**—Happy clients come as a result of happy employees. Begin with a commitment to your employees and your clients will feel the benefit. Be an employer of choice, and create an army of advocates.

- **Overhire talented recruiters**—If you're going to skew heavily in any one area of recruitment, you need to recruit highly skilled recruiters. Do not fall into the trap of underestimating the significance of the war for talent. Great recruiters will have a direct and long-lasting impact on your business.
- **ABR**—Always be recruiting, in every way, by everyone. Build an internal referral program, and recognize those who bring talent forward. Every employee needs to be an ambassador of your brand and culture.
- **Be personally involved**—I have been involved in every hiring decision made within my areas of responsibility in every organization that I have been involved with (thousands of people). When you are the leader, it is your team, your culture, and your vision. There is too much at stake to trust this process solely to others. Nothing can shape an organization's culture like great people, and nothing can disrupt it like a missed hire. I want opinions, but I need to be one of them. In order to ensure alignment, commit to being intimately involved in the hiring process.

Over the balance of this chapter, I will share recruitment techniques that will allow you to properly target, prioritize, and vet talent. As a leader, I am a firm believer that if you don't make mistakes, you are not taking enough chances. However, the one area in which you must do everything in your power to avoid mistakes is recruiting talent. Nothing is costlier than bringing in a new employee who doesn't fit culturally and who doesn't bring the will and skill necessary to excel in his or her role. This must be your priority. Have your hand in as many stages of talent recruitment as is humanly possible. Recruitment is about both parties. It is not about a leader finding talent. It is about a company finding a person and a person finding a company. It must be right for both parties, or it will fail. Be open and honest with the candidate throughout the process. Let him or her know that the decision must be right for both the company and the individual. This will result in an immediate reaction from the candidate that you care and that you are committed to creating a win-win situation in the process. It will bring forward a human element in a process that all too often is lacking warmth.

Prior to interviewing

- In chapter 1, we defined the attributes we seek when hiring talent. Above all else, you must identify what it is that you want, and then you must go out and find it. What attributes are important to achieving at the levels you seek? What attributes are important to maintaining and improving upon your current corporate culture? This is a great exercise, as this will help shape the character of your organization. Take this exercise seriously, and do not prioritize experience over these attributes. Nothing is more important. Attributes trump experience every day. Attributes shape culture. Ensure that you are aligned tightly with your recruitment team on these attributes. Alignment is critical to ensuring efficiency and a seamless approach to the process.
- Take a look at all job descriptions for each role. Earlier, we discussed creating your organizational

brand. Think of your job descriptions as the initial view into your business. Are your job descriptions whispering, or are they screaming out? They should be less about the specific role and more about what you stand for, what you believe in, your vision, and your values. State your *why* above all else. This is your brand. This is what you want to be known for. Go into this exercise with the intention of wowing talent. Use video testimonials from current employees and clients, and speak to the applicants. The difference between a standard job description and a fully branded and passionate job description will make a marked difference in the talent that you eventually secure. Take your time on your job descriptions. By investing time and attention, you will move viewers to applicants and applicants to employees.

- With advancements in technology, you no longer have to rely solely on the phone and the recruiter's initial impression of that discussion. I have worked with some amazing recruiters, but we have often differed in our opinions of a particular applicant, as our biases have been shaped by our experiences. To eliminate those differences of opinion, use a video application process. I have had success using the HireVue platform. Identify ten questions specific to that particular role and have them prerecorded by senior leaders and respected team members. Incorporate the link into your job description, and wait for the applications to roll in. The recruiter will then eliminate any applicants who do not fit the role and pass those remaining to the hiring manager and the head of the division to review. Each question will be graded, and the applicant will either be moved forward or rejected. This is a great first step in the recruitment process. If you are hiring for remote roles, HireVue can be used for the formal interview with the hiring manager. Again, the interview will be recorded and reviewed by all parties involved in the hiring process. Here's the potential interviewing process:

1. The candidate records the ten-question interview application and submits it for consideration.
2. The recruiter does the initial review and forwards appropriate applicants to the designated point person (you).
3. The point person reviews the application to ensure that the candidate is solid and passes the person along to the hiring manager to schedule a formal interview: recorded if the position is remote; in person if the position is local.
4. If the interview is recorded, the point person (you) receives and reviews the interview.
5. If both parties like the candidate, the point person (you) schedules a final cultural interview.
6. All involved parties discuss the candidate and make a decision.

- Conduct a personality profile. Prior to the first face-to-face interview (remote or in person), have the candidate take a personality profile. There are many different profiling tools on the market; find the one that aligns most closely to the role you are looking to fill. I have had success using both HireSelect (Criteria Corp) and SalesDrive. Personality profiles are not the be-all and end-all within the actual recruitment stage, but they are certainly an important part of the overall process. While they can be a bit unnerving for the candidate, they can uncover certain characteristics that may align well, or not so well, with the role. Either way, they provide you with questions to ask, based on the candidate's score in given categories. As an additional checkpoint, be sure to take the test yourself and have your top ten performers take the test as well. Combine the scores, and you will have a view into what an optimal score may look like by category. You can then plot the candidate's score within each category and note the alignment with the top-performing employees currently in that role. This provides a glimpse into the candidate's potential success in the role. Again, this is only one element of the process and is not intended to be weighted more heavily than other, more critical components.

- As with any meeting or sales call, preparation plays a key role. Take your time, and study the candidate. Take a look at his or her previous experience and note any gaps between roles. If you see any, be sure to ask about them in the interview. If there are several gaps, this could be an indication of consistent dismissals or simply bad timing/luck. Lastly, be sure to review the candidate's social media presence. This will tell you a lot about how he or she carries him- or herself, what he or she believes in, and if his or her character and values align with those of your organization. I have passed on many candidates after reviewing their Facebook and Twitter presences.

During the interview

- There are four types of interview questions: traditional, behavioral, situational, and motivational.
  - **Traditional**—"Tell me about yourself," "What are your strengths and weaknesses?," and "How would your boss describe you?" fall into the category of traditional questions.
  - **Behavioral**—Most commonly, behavioral questions begin with phrases like "Tell me about a time when…" or "Describe a situation in which…" They require the candidate to share how he or she would behave in a given situation that could arise in the role for which they are interviewing.
  - **Situational**—In situational interview questions, candidates are asked to describe how they would handle themselves in given situations. These questions are designed to test the candidate's analytical and problem-solving skills.
  - **Motivational**—These questions are designed to pull out the candidate's key motivators, drivers, and passions.
- Depending on how many interviews are scheduled, you could assign lines of questioning to each interviewer. For example, one interviewer could focus on behavioral questions, while another could target more traditional questions. Assuming a relatively

flat interviewing hierarchy (two or three people), I would recommend a blended approach. I have a list of approximately twenty questions that I like to ask. Here are a few:

o **Tell me your story**—I like to understand how candidates view themselves. Do they speak personally? Do they share their inspirations and accomplishments? Do they share what is important to them or just the jobs they've held? This also provides a view into their preparation. This is a pretty standard question, so if a candidate is not locked in on his or her personal story, how can I expect him or her to internalize my company's value proposition?

o **What research have you done on our company, and what are your impressions thus far?**—Preparation leads to success. In what could arguably be a candidate's most important meeting ever, my hope is that he or she has done his or her homework and can articulate our mission and vision profoundly. I have ended interviews after this question when the candidate was not passionate and informed. I am respectful when ending an interview, explaining why intellectual curiosity is such an important part of our culture and that, if he or she came ill prepared to understand what we do and why we do it, we cannot continue down the path. This is a teaching moment.

o **What interests you most about this position?**—Again, I want to see that the candidate has done research and is passionate about this role and his or her ability to find success. The best interviewees share elements of the job description and state how their experiences and talents align with each of those criteria.

o **What is your general attitude toward life?**—This is a big one. This will tell you what is important to a candidate and what he or she values most.

o **Who are the biggest influencers in your life?**—This question will give you a view of a candidate's mentors, be they parents, previous employers, or public figures. Be sure to understand the *why* behind whomever the candidate shares as his or her biggest influence. Again, this will say a lot about what is important to him or her.

o **What is your proudest achievement, personally or professionally?**—I need to see a distinct achievement orientation. With this answer, ideally you will see the pride and passion shine through.

o **What one thing would you change about your past/current job?**—The answer to this question will provide a view into a candidate's level of positivity. While I am looking for the candidate to state a weakness of their previous/current role, more specifically, I am looking for how he or she goes about describing the opportunity to change it. If there is a deep level of negativity, I will shy away.

▪ During the interview, I engage the candidate in a couple of exercises. I've found that breaking up the interview allows for a deeper level of engagement. I write the following terms on a big whiteboard, and I ask the candidate to rank them from one to five, one being most applicable or important. As I did with the personality profile, I have asked my top ten performers to rate these items as well, allowing for a comparison set of already-successful employees. The goal is to reduce the risk of hiring the wrong candidate as much as possible, and having three comparison groups assists in accomplishing this goal. This is a deliberately difficult task. It allows you to view the way the candidate goes about determining the rankings, as well as his or her conviction about the outcome. Identify your own five or six criteria, specific to your organization's needs. The exercise is worthwhile. Here are the two exercises. Put the five choices on the board and ask them to rank them from one to five:

o **Qualities that you possess**—Being organized, strong work ethic, perseverance, passion, ability to handle rejection.

o **What motivates you?**—Making money, being the top performer, autonomy, growth, recognition.

Following the interview

At the end of the interview, I state the following: "Mary, we've covered a lot during our time together today. There's a lot to digest. I'd like to ask that you think about our time together, and if you decide that you are interested in moving forward, I'd like for you to send me an e-mail before your head hits the pillow tonight, stating why you are the right candidate and why you want to be a part of our organization. Your e-mail can be as long and creative as you'd like to make it; as long as I get it before midnight tonight, we'll be good."

This exercise accomplishes several things. First, I want to see Mary's level of commitment. I want to see her thought process, the level of depth that she puts into this exercise, and the creativity of her approach. I've been blown away by some and underwhelmed by others. Second, I want to see if she goes through the process of aligning her skill sets to the needs of the role. As the exercise specifically asks her to state why she is the right candidate and why she wants to be part of the organization, I want to see if she can then follow instructions, and I want to identify the level of passion she has around the fit. This is Mary's selling moment. I need to see enthusiasm. Third, I want to see how she writes. Much of our communication, both internally with fellow employees and externally with clients, requires a written approach. Poor grammar and misspelling are knockouts. If Mary doesn't have enough respect for the process to proofread something as important as this, how will she communicate with our clients? Finally, I want to see if she can meet a deadline. I specifically state midnight to ensure that she understands that the exercise is time sensitive. Believe it or not, I've had candidates send me their responses after midnight, and I have passed on them. Some I've really liked, but I am in a deadline business, and if a candidate cannot meet as important a deadline as an interview determining his or her professional path, how can I trust him or her to meet quotas and internal deadlines?

Be sure to ask the candidate for five references and have him or her actively engaged in the process (sharing contacts and reaching out to those contacts). Based on the candidate's reaction to this exercise, you will have a glimpse into his or her personal confidence and credibility. Hesitation is likely not a good sign. If he or she delivers a list of friends or peer coworkers, that's likely not a good sign either. I like to see a list of several supervisors. That tells me that the candidate was respected and that his or her results were solid. Use your judgment if the individual has been with their company for an extended period of time and the organization is not aware the individual is interviewing elsewhere. Obviously, this would pose an obstacle in providing supervisory reference checks and would require your judgment and potential flexibility.

Be sure that the hiring manager conducts these reference checks personally. I am finding that reference checking is becoming more of a check-the-box task when it needs to be prioritized. I've been fooled many times in interviews. By prioritizing the reference-checking process, you can gain clarity around any remaining items or concerns. Enter the call with well-crafted questions and a clear understanding of what you want to accomplish during the call. Be prepared, as some companies are reluctant to share information beyond dates of employment. In these instances, pull out all that you can. In addition, LinkedIn is a powerful platform. Depending on the depth of your network, you will likely be able to find a first- or second-degree connection who can give you a quality "back-door" reference. I tend to find more value in back-door references than in self-provided ones.

As the overall recruitment process is so important to the success of an organization, I'd recommend building an internal document identifying the hiring "batting average" for each recruiter, hiring manager, and yourself. Some people are exceedingly good at identifying talent, while others struggle in this area. Through an understanding of each person's conversion rate, best practices will emerge, and once you identify who has the best feel for recruiting talent, you can then cross-train and lift your success rate across the board. Talent will make or break an organization. By putting together a strong recruitment process and committing the resources and focus there, your organization will be in a tremendous position to thrive. Talent begets talent. Great people want to be around other great people. By recruiting the best talent, you will attract the best talent. Commit to being an employer of choice. It all begins with a strong focus on your recruitment process. Remember, the organization will flex as you flex. If hiring talent is important to you, it will become important to all and with talent, amazing things will happen.

CHAPTER 19

TOPGRADING

The term *topgrading* is most often associated with Jack Welch, from his days as CEO of General Electric. The concept of topgrading came about as a result of Welch pressing his leaders to make decisions on lower-performing employees. He was frustrated that so many leaders would avoid dealing with talent challenges, often hiding the lower performers rather than addressing, investing, improving, or displacing them. He felt that there were several reasons for this:

- Leaders felt that it would demotivate the person and potentially cause disruption among the troops.
- Leaders felt that most often a new hire would perform no better than the person who was displaced.
- Leaders felt that something was better than nothing, as they believed that a tenured employee would contribute more than a new and ramping employee in the near term.

Welch mentioned that he spent nearly 50 percent of his time as CEO on talent issues. In the 1980s, GE brought in Brad Smart, who developed and helped train thousands of leaders at GE on the practice of topgrading. Topgrading extends far beyond simply replacing lower-performing employees, encompassing many key areas and permeating the entire organization: hiring, promoting, coaching, retaining talent, and developing succession planning. By definition, topgrading is an evaluative method for identifying the most highly qualified candidate for a particular job position. The principle involves identifying and developing A talent and coaching B and C talent to become A players. Again, a common misconception is that topgrading is primarily focused on displacement of poor performers. While displacement is certainly a part of the process, topgrading is truly about developing talent and placing the right person in a role in which he or she can flourish. Upon implementation of topgrading at GE, Bill Conaty, former longtime head of HR, estimated that GE enjoyed an 80 percent success rate in hiring leaders within the company. That is an amazingly high success rate.

In his book *Topgrading: How Leading Companies Win by Hiring, Coaching, and Keeping the Best People*, Brad Smart outlines twelve competencies of A players:

- **Resourcefulness**—The A player knows how to leverage those around him or her to accomplish goals.
- **Ability to select A players and redeploy B/C players**—The leader can address performance challenges respectfully and does not shy away from tough

conversations or doing what's right for the person and the organization.

- **Passion**—The A player exudes a sense of purpose and a drive to excel and assist others in their development.
- **Integrity**—The A player can be trusted to do the right thing at all times.
- **Ambition**—The A player has an eye on the future and wants to accept additional responsibility.
- **Political savvy**—The A player stays away from drama, chatter, and managing upward.
- **Adaptability**—The A player can adjust to change and embraces it openly.
- **Ability to be a team builder**—The A player is focused on building a cohesive unit, driven by the success of the organization rather than his or her own success.
- **Ability to be a team player**—The A player looks for success for all, working well among departments and across channels.
- **Track record**—The A player is consistent in his or her delivery of results, working through challenges and finding a way to perform at a high level, regardless of what is in front of him or her.
- **Intelligence**—The A player has an aptitude for learning and the ability to contribute.
- **Likability**—The A player relates well to people and shows respect to all.

Brad outlines the key attributes for top coaches from a leadership standpoint:

- **Partnership**—Top coaches truly care about their people and their success. They are engaged, interested, respected, and respectful.
- **Promoting autonomy**—Top coaches provide a platform for self-discovery by learning through doing.
- **Positivity**—Top coaches are passionate, inspiring, and enthusiastic and consistently practice recognition and reinforcement.
- **Trustworthiness**—Top coaches can be counted on to follow through. They are open and honest and do not overpromise.
- **Caring**—Top coaches are empathetic, compassionate, and sincere.
- **Patience**—Top coaches listen, understand, are tolerant, and are reasonable.
- **Results orientation**—Top coaches can be counted on to deliver on goals, expectations, and commitments.
- **Perception**—Top coaches have the ability to view a situation and understand, assess, and react accordingly.
- **Authoritativeness**—Top coaches are knowledgeable, wise, and clear in their feedback.
- **Active listening**—Top coaches clarify, summarize, and react accordingly.

Entering into the full topgrading process takes commitment at all levels. At a minimum, I'd recommend that you look at three distinct areas: hiring, promoting, and displacing. In the last chapter, we discussed questions and processes for improving your recruiting results. Let's take a look at the second area—promoting.

I have had the opportunity to work within several great organizations in my career. Entering each of those organizations, I found a common theme: employees are unclear on the process of advancing their careers. In fact, in each of my professional career changes, there was no clearly articulated advancement or succession process. When we talk about what employees want, growth is consistently a key desire, yet they are unclear about how to go about this process. While it is certainly a challenge to project future needs, it is imperative that we openly develop and identify a process for the future.

There are several steps that you need to take:

- **Share the future vision**—In previous chapters, we discussed the need for transparency with regard to a company's vision. By clearly and openly sharing the plan—monthly or, at a minimum, quarterly—we can begin to map out future personnel needs. Call those out as you share the vision. This will provide a view for advancement for those who are interested. After communicating these needs, leaders should reiterate them in team calls and one-on-one meetings.
- **Share the process**—In all-company vision calls, team meetings, and one-on-one meetings, leaders need to share the timing and the process for potential advancement. Share the criteria that will be reviewed, as well as the weightings, or emphasis, that will be placed on each decision category. Work to base more than 50 percent on objective measures. A heavier subjective skew leads to feelings of favoritism. The more metrics you can bring to the decision process, the better. Here's an example:
  - o ***Place 30 percent decision weight based on rankings***— We will discuss rankings in upcoming chapters,

but having a system that normalizes the field is important.

o *Place 20 percent decision weight based on face-to-face interviews with yourself and two or three additional interviewers*—Depending on the level of the role, these could be fellow executives.

o *Place 20 percent decision weight based on a 360 review*—This will allow you to understand how the candidate is viewed by his or her subordinates (if applicable), peers, and supervisor.

o *Place 10 percent decision weight based on a project to follow*—An example would be to have interested parties work independently on a challenge that the team is facing.

o *Place 10 percent decision weight based on the past two years' performance reviews*—Take this one step further and speak with previous reviewers to gain additional insight.

o *Place 10 percent decision weight based on HireVue ten interview questions*—Utilizing this platform, put together ten questions that apply to the role and have the candidates record their responses.

Build a matrix to track the candidates, grading their success in each of the six recognized areas. This allows for you to be very open and consistent throughout the process, alleviating any questions about favoritism.

The final area of topgrading is the most challenging, painful, and disruptive—displacement. In my thirty-plus-year leadership career, I have had to displace many employees, and every time, as much as I realize that it is necessary, it is personal, and it is painful. Every time an employee is displaced, I feel it deep in my core. I feel that I personally let that person down. I view displacement as failure on my part. I eventually get through it by telling myself a few things:

- **This person has value, just not here**—We put an enormous amount of time into our professions. If we are failing, we struggle to find happiness. And when we're not happy, we have a tendency to bring that into other areas of our lives. I am helping guide this person toward something in which he or she will thrive, find reward, and be happy.

- **If I'm truly crowning the company, I must fulfill my obligation**—As business leaders, we must acknowledge whom we serve. We serve our clients, our people, and our organizations. We have a responsibility that extends beyond ourselves and our teams; it extends to all employees. If I neglect my responsibility to place the best possible team on the field each day, I am putting the livelihoods of other employees at risk. By making poor choices, I could put my organization at risk, which would in turn place every employee at risk.

- **I have given my all, and I have been fair in my assessment**—At this point, I have invested a great deal of time and effort into this individual. I have been clear in my expectations, I have listened to his or her needs, and I have helped in every way that I can. I have graded his or her results consistently with those of his or her peers and have been open in my communication throughout the process. I have been respectful.

As painful as this process is, it is necessary. The key is to be respectful and open throughout the process and avoid surprises at all costs. If the person shows will, work with him or her. Work to develop his or her skill. People with *skill* are easy to find. Those with *will* are much more difficult to locate. Attitude and aptitude are attributes that A players exhibit. If we are working toward a team made up of A players, we must not compromise when it comes to the need for these attributes and the expectation that anything short of this will not be part of the go-forward plan. "A or no way" needs to be our mantra.

Be sure to put a process in place to track your employee churn reasons and review them monthly. Track the hiring manager, original date of hire, termination date, tenure, whether the employee was terminated or resigned, and the employee's rank (if in a ranked system). This will help you identify the effectiveness in your hiring and onboarding processes, your training, and effectiveness by leader.

Last note on topgrading: Do not tolerate a lack of will or respect. There is no gray area when it comes to doing the right thing. Regardless if he or she is your best employee, bad attitudes and disrespectful behavior need to be dealt with swiftly and decisively. You will be judged based on your action or inaction. Do the right thing by your organization and your employees. Be consistent, be respectful, hold high expectations, and never settle when it comes to hiring and keeping talent. With great people, amazing things happen. You owe it to yourself, your employees, and the entire organization to put the absolute best talent on the field every day.

CHAPTER 20

ONBOARDING

I 'd like to start this chapter by taking you back to your last couple of career moves. Think about the interview process. Things were good. Things felt right. Everyone put forth his or her best self, rarely showing blemishes. Both parties felt really good about each other, and the mutual decision was made to move forward. You walked into your current boss's office and resigned. He or she may have been stunned and may have even made a counteroffer, but you stood your ground, because you believed in this new organization. Leading up to day one, you told your entire family and all of your friends about this new opportunity. You were excited, and you were fired up. And then came the first day.

I have had the good fortune of working with many really good companies, a couple of start-ups, several in high-growth mode, and a couple in the Fortune 500. All but one of them missed the mark in onboarding me. In fact, I would say that there was no real onboarding in most of them. In several cases, there wasn't even any formalized training. I'm sad to say that this is closer to the current state of affairs than where I am going to suggest that you need to be.

As I see it, there are four stages of onboarding:

- **Offer onboarding**—This is your moment to set the tone for your relationship. First, the hiring manager, and not HR, needs to make the offer. This is going to be your person. You need to share your enthusiasm and passion directly. You also need to be very clear about the offer and sell it! Keep in mind that this candidate has likely been interviewing elsewhere, and someone else may be making an offer to him or her as well. Another company might even be making an offer the same day you are making yours. You have to be on your A game in order to secure A talent. The candidate is buying you above all else. Visualize the conversation, have your talking points written out, and walk through them.

- **Prestart onboarding**—This is the time between the candidate's acceptance of your offer and his or her start date. This is the time when you need to be sensitive to your surroundings. Again, the candidate was likely interviewing elsewhere, and offers will continue to come his or her way. You can bet that if this person is good, other companies are still speaking with him or her. I have seen numerous situations, more than I care to admit, in which people have bailed in this prestart period. The best way to offset the counterattacks is through engagement. Send a handwritten note with a gift. I like to send company swag (jacket, T-shirt, pens, notepads, etc.). The key is to surprise and delight. Maybe send flowers to his or her spouse. This is the time to start personalizing your relationship. Then, if someone else comes calling prestart, you've already won over the new hire's heart.

- **First-day onboarding**—Your entire company should know when new people are starting and in what roles they will be working, and they should be ready to welcome new people on day one. Have a sign up front welcoming the new people, and decorate their desks. Have their equipment ready and their desks fully stocked. I know this sounds a bit childish, but I have personally seen it work beautifully. When a new person arrives, the receptionist should welcome him or her by name, by coming out from behind the desk and shaking his or her hand. The new supervisor should be on alert and come up front at the time that the new person is due to arrive. This is the time for a true first impression. The interview doesn't count, at this point. This is all about the new hire's career and the choice that he or she made. Help confirm that it was a great choice. If you have set training and weekly/monthly all-company calls scheduled, I'd recommend that you align those days. It would be optimal if you could introduce the new folks to the entire company on their first day. Bring in food and make it a celebration. Treat this first day with great passion and enthusiasm. It will make a huge difference in their initial perceptions of your business, winning over their hearts, and influencing their eventual contributions to your overall organizational culture.

- **Ramp onboarding**—Onboarding should not be treated as a one-and-done event. New employees are learning for an extended period of time, and after they are trained, they can fall into bad habits unless there is a commitment to their long-term success. I recommend a ninety-day onboarding time line. Habits are formed over a period of time. Invest in ensuring that your new hires form the right habits, which will contribute to their success in their careers.

When entering into this part of the process, we must first understand that onboarding and training are related but not to be confused with each other. They have different goals and sets of standards. Onboarding focuses on attitude (passion/will), while training primarily focuses on aptitude (skill). We must also lose the term *probationary period* when referencing the first three months of an employee's tenure with an organization. It blows me away that this term is still used. To reference such a positive event as bringing a new employee into the "family" with a negative term like *probation* is very one sided and lacks the sensitivity and positive reinforcement needed during such an important moment in an individual's career. We need to enter into any relationship with a focus on and commitment to a positive outcome. Can you imagine looking at the first three months of a marriage as a probationary period? Both a marriage and a career require engagement and commitment. In both of them, we need to be *all in.*

To further emphasize the need for a committed onboarding process, I'd like to offer the following research. In 2014, BambooHR studied and reported on the onboarding process, specifically what new hires want during onboarding:

- New hires want their managers, not HR, to take the lead.
- In their first week, 76 percent of new hires want on-the-job training; 73 percent want to understand company policies; 59 percent want a tour, tools, and to understand procedures; and 56 percent want a mentor.
- In the first six months, 31 percent of new hires quit, with 16 percent quitting in the first week and 21 percent within the first three months.
- The top five reasons that new hires leave early are changing direction on work type, being given different work than they expected, feeling that their bosses were "jerks," not receiving enough training, and finding that their new workplaces were not "fun" environments.
- New hires want clear guidelines, effective training, a friendly environment, more recognition, and more attention.

So how do we go about ensuring a successful onboarding and allowing our new employees to feel welcomed and part of the team?

- **Make onboarding a priority**—As the leader, you need to be intimately involved with and committed to successful onboarding. Be clear with your entire workforce that onboarding is a priority and that everyone owns it together.
- **Form an onboarding committee**—The more brains, the better. Involve your staff in coming up with a plan that will help new hires feel welcomed and important.

- **Engage prestart**—Just because somebody signed an offer letter doesn't mean that he or she will show up on day one. You need to keep earning his or her trust and respect at every stage. Remember that great people are always being courted. Do your best to offset any competitive advances.
- **Every employee owns onboarding**—We all own culture, and every new employee either advances our culture or diminishes it. We must all shape culture together.
- **A game on day one**—Everybody is committed to a stellar first day for new employees. We either confirm that they made a great choice, or we begin to lose them.
- **Commit to ninety-day onboarding**—One day, one week, or one month is not enough time. A strong mentorship program coupled with semimonthly check-in meetings will lead to a new hire feeling a strong sense of commitment, ownership, engagement, and fulfillment and lessen his or her propensity to depart.
- **Ask for feedback**—Ask all new hires what they feel they are receiving well and what they would like to receive in addition to what they have received through their respective onboarding processes. This can be done informally (one-on-one check-ins) and formally (thirty-, sixty-, and ninety-day surveys).

CHAPTER 21

TRAINING

CFO asks CEO: "What happens if we invest in developing our people and then they leave us?"
CEO responds to CFO: "What happens if we don't and they stay?"

In order to build an inspiring culture, we must be intentional about our willingness to invest in our truly differentiating asset—our people. Often, organizations view training as an expense rather than an investment, and when a company falls on challenging times, training is among the first items to be cut. My hope is that by the end of this chapter, you will realize that investing in your people means investing in their development and that training is an absolute necessity in your organization. Allow me to share two primary reasons why training must be a top priority:

1. **Untrained employees are unhappy employees**—One of the primary influences on employee happiness is

being a part of a culture focused on people—one in which the organization invests in the development of its staff. Invest in your people, or they will find someone who will.

2. **Untrained employees are unproductive employees—** Training keeps employees sharp. Challenge spurs emotions and stirs intellectual curiosity. Training must be relevant. It must be meaningful. It must be purposeful. Training will enhance productivity and results.

Abraham Lincoln was quoted as saying, "Give me six hours to chop down a tree, and I will spend the first four sharpening the axe." This quote is specifically applicable to people development. We preach productivity and metrics, and we expect the productivity and metrics to continue, based solely on the intentional focus on those activities. I am as metrics driven as leaders come, but I've come to realize that as a stand-alone lever, activity will plateau and likely diminish if all you do is focus on that activity. You will also be viewed as a micromanager. The only way a metrics-driven organization can flourish is by investing in people through committed training—in essence, sharpening the axe.

Once the commitment to invest in your people by investing in training is made, there are a couple of things to remember:

Training investment and development

- **Build in house**—Often companies invest in outside, rather than in-house, training. A committed process is owned from the inside out. Either you are a training-minded organization, or you are not. Hiring an outside company, rather than building from within, means you are halfway committed. While I believe in the need to utilize outside organizations to polish up specific skill sets, your general, consistent, day-to-day training needs to come from your team.

- **Handpick your training team**—A common mistake involves taking the best people and making them trainers and managers. In many instances, this is appropriate; however, in many instances, it is not. Just because someone is a great individual contributor does not mean that he or she will have the passion or talent to develop others. You must be involved in the selection process while keeping in mind that those you select will be the face of your organization. They will be developing the talent of the future for your company. Because they will be owning this responsibility, do not rely solely on an interview or a resume. Give the candidates a topic and ask them to prepare a fifteen-minute presentation. Note their poise, their attention to detail, and their confidence. Look for creativity, passion, and believability. Envision yourself as a new hire, and ask yourself, "Am I impressed that this is the face of the organization that I have just chosen to join?" The answer must be an emphatic *yes!*
- **Invest in your training team**—Get the best, and pay them well. The influence that they will have on the future of your organization cannot be overstated. Great trainers move businesses.

- **Train the trainers**—If you have a training background, be intimately involved in crafting credible curriculum. If you don't, hire outside trainers to work with your trainers in their content development. There are many elements that make up a great training team. At the forefront are content and delivery. Being strong in one without strength in the other will lead to failure. The content will only be received as well as it is being delivered. Great trainers with poor content and poor trainers with great content lead to flat outcomes. The size of your training team will determine if you need both a content and a delivery team or if you will need to find trainers capable of both, which can be a bit more challenging. Either way, you need powerful delivery wrapped around powerful content.
- **Emphasize "discovery"**—Specifically in regard to sales, nothing is more important than slowing down the "race" to the close and focusing on the needs of the client. Sales is all about asking questions, uncovering needs, building connections, and easing pain. This must be emphasized and internalized by leaders and trainers. This needs to be a part of your sales fabric and trained in a disciplined and intentional way with your existing staff and new hires. It will be absolutely critical to your organizational success.
- **Inspect what you expect**—Prior to any sessions being delivered to an audience, they must first be delivered to you to tweak and approve. Believe me, this is too important and can have too big of an impact (either way) to trust that it will be developed and delivered to

your liking. Review all new-hire training weeks prior to implementation and be sure to adjust after every class.

- **Meet with the training team weekly**—Sit in on the team's weekly sessions and brainstorm alongside the team members. Develop ideas together. Illustrate your commitment to each of them and to the process. Many of these folks will be future leaders in your organization. It is helpful to get an up-close and personal view into their thought processes and intellect.

- **Lengthen new-hire training**—Regardless of how long you believe training should last, double it. If you believe it should be a week, make it two weeks. An extra week or two will make a world of difference in your understanding of whether a new hire is a good fit, while also allowing for additional time to assist him or her in reducing his or her future ramp to success. The longer you train a new hire, the more productive and confident he or she will become. Fast starts lead to great careers.

- **Set high expectations of the trainers**—We need our training teams to understand that they will have a big hand in the future success of the company. Challenge them to stretch. Challenge them to understand that everyone they work with is their customer and that they will find reward (and be judged) based on how their trainees perform.

- **Compensate the trainers for the success of the new hires**—We will discuss this at more length when we discuss compensation, but the trainer's compensation must be tied to the successful ramp on the new hires. You will get what you choose to compensate. If you believe in investing in a strong ramp for new hires, pay for that at both the new-hire and trainer levels. One thing is for certain: the trainers will ensure successful ramps for new hires if you pay them for that result.

Let's take a look at the core deliverables from the training team—most notably, new-hire training and continued education.

New-hire training

- **Thank and welcome them genuinely**—First things first: *thank* the group for choosing you. This is a two-way street. Gratitude goes both ways. They likely had choices, and they have placed their futures in your hands. Let them know that you appreciate that and will not let them down. Relate to the tough decision they had to make and let them know that you understand the responsibility that you have to them and their families. This will go a long way. Also, explain that from this day forward, they can be anyone that they want to be, much like the day they graduated from high school or college. What each person did prior to this class got them to this point, but it won't matter going forward. The only thing that matters is what they choose to do and who they choose to become, from this point forward.

- **Engage them actively**—At the start, have fun with the introductions. Map out several questions, with a couple of them being fun (first concert, favorite movie, passion outside of work, etc.). Bring the personalities out (yours and theirs), and break down their guard. Set the tone for the training: they are going to learn while having fun at the same time.

- **Share the plan**—Lay out the agenda day by day, so they know what they can expect. This illustrates two distinct things: you cared enough to put time in on their behalf, and you take this very seriously. What is about to happen is not an accident. It is a plan that is intended to allow them to flourish.

- **Set expectations**—Explain what the new hires can expect from you during training and, more importantly, from the organization after training. Let them know that there is a commitment to their success, further confirming that they made a great decision.

- **Start big**—Throughout day one, have each executive come in and present to the team. There are no "off-the-cuff" presentations; they should be formal and well orchestrated, each with a specific theme and purpose, centered on the values of the organization. They are to be delivered passionately and with an intended, powerful, and personal message. The CEO/founder leads off (after thank yous, welcomes, intros, and agenda) and tells the story of how the organization was founded and the *why* behind the organization's existence. The CEO emphasizes the importance of the company's mission, vision, and values. Each executive should have a creative deck, including proper messaging and creative imagery. The organization is being judged heavily on day one. The goal is for each new hire to call his or her family at day's end and share his or her excitement for the new organization.

- **Get the flow right**—Strike a balance between content and engagement. Stay away from heavy module work at the start and spread the heavy content out as much as possible. Optimal learning takes place when both sides of the brain are working. Challenge the team emotionally and strategically.

- **Be here now**—No phones, no distractions. Everybody needs to be *all in* on this career decision. All parties own their success. Plan lots of breaks, but when in the room, we are locked and loaded. This goes for trainers and guests also. Everyone must respect the learning environment.

- **Train values**—Beyond the executive presentations, which covered the values, test for understanding of the values. It's that important. Hang banners in the room to remind everyone what the organization believes in and stands for.

- **Bring in guests beyond the executive team**—HR, IT, and payroll will all play a role. In addition, bring in top-performing individual contributors to speak about what they love about their positions and the company. Again, this will serve to fuel the passion and ignite the visceral side of the new hires. Help them believe that they are part of the solution and will play a major role in creating something truly special.

- **Role-play**—Scripts are an important part of any customer-facing departments. I highly recommend that you capture the right messaging and expect that every person in a given role be able to recite that before he or she graduates from training. I would also recommend that you send it to the new team members prior to starting new-hire training (in written, pop-up, and audio/video form) and ask them to familiarize themselves with the content. Every day, work on the scripting together and individually, explaining the *why* behind each piece and how to deliver. Scripting is not a bad thing, so don't shy away. Businesses need continuity in messaging, and by creating scripts, you are able to control the flow of content and keep it delivered in a consistent and organized way. There is a misconception that scripts sound like scripts. Last time I checked, every actor has a script and has to memorize it verbatim. I've seen a lot of movies, and none of them sound scripted. The director has a vision for the film, and that takes everyone delivering the messaging in the proper way. In our professional lives, we need to do the same: control messaging. During the first half of the first day, two trainers should perform a role play, so everyone can see how it should look. At the end of day one, ask for a volunteer. Leaders usually step forward. Practice in break-out groups every day, and at the end of the week, have a final videotaped role play that will be sent to the hiring manager.

- **Provide nightly updates**—The training team needs to send nightly updates on the progress of each new hire to the heads of the departments to whom each person will ultimately report. The executive needs to see progress and get involved as needed for those slow to progress or appearing disengaged.
- **Fail fast**—If you made a mistake in hiring one of the trainees, have the lead trainer address the issue first. Open and honest communication is imperative. As

with anything else, it's not *what* you say but *how* you say it. Be respectful but direct. State your expectations and where the trainee is falling shy of those expectations. We are not trying to bring anyone down; we simply believe in transparent communication (stated during values discussion), and this is where we practice it. Remember, we will be judged based on our action or inaction. We are being judged during every day of training. We will lose the trust of the other new hires if we choose to avoid dealing with sensitive situations or challenging trainees. As the leader of the organization, be prepared to get involved should things worsen after the lead trainer conversation.

- **Go off-site several nights together**—Plan fun group dinners and outings, and invite executives to join. We are creating a culture of "work hard, play hard," so let's go out and create some memorable experiences. Stay away from the standard pizza and do something like guacamole making, sushi rolling, pasta making or go to a ball game. We want to personalize the training experience and get to know people on a personal level. Avoid being cheap here. Invest in the people and show them a good time, as they will be working hard. That said, control the alcohol flow. We don't want to create an environment that feels like a fraternity. We want to have fun, but we want to avoid crossing any lines or placing people in uncomfortable situations.

- **Have a graduation ceremony**—Very informally, invite the entire office to meet for cake and graduation late on the final day. Play "Pomp and Circumstance," and have each graduate come up, shake hands with the lead trainer and executive, accept a certificate, and take a picture. This is *not* intended to be formal or stiff but more fun than anything else. Take a group picture, and then have some cake. It's a nice way to cap off a challenging and stressful week of learning. Send the team picture out to the entire company, welcoming the new class.

- **Be aggressive in goal setting**—If training sales folks, share the current high bar set by previous training classes and ask them to commit to surpassing the prior record. Give a $50 gift card to anyone who sets a new record. Also, give prizes for the top two people in the class ($250 and $100 gift cards). Set high goals and ask people to surpass them. Have them select a training class team name and send out nightly updates of their progress. At the end of a two-week incentive period, send a note out to the entire company, recognizing individual and team successes.

- **Survey and tweak**—Survey the trainees at the end of their class, and then again after thirty days. Understand where you did well but, more importantly, where you can improve. The goal is not to judge the trainers; the goal is to consistently improve, class after class. We must avoid defensiveness here. We must make continuous improvement a value that we all embrace.

Continued training

- **Twice-monthly development training**—Have the training team develop content for continuing education for every role. It is relevant. It is pertinent. Again, all content development must be reviewed by the leader to ensure alignment with company initiatives and relevance to the specific roles. Training must be role specific to ensure engagement and maximize development.

- **Recertify all salespeople on the script**—Nearly every time that a salesperson struggles, it is because activities are down, messaging is askew, or a combination of both. In order to *ensure* alignment in messaging, we must *certify* alignment in messaging. While this will be met with some level of resistance ("I don't follow the script because I'm the top rep."), turn it into a fun competition, complete with prizes and recognition (maybe a trip for the winner and his or her guest). The company and clients will win as a result. Whether it's the top rep or the bottom rep, message alignment is imperative, and everyone, including managers, should be held to the same standards.
- **Tap into your A players**—We will discuss best practices in the next chapter, but by utilizing your best individual contributors, you will ensure that the content will be highly relevant.

As I stated at the start of this chapter, training takes commitment and investment. You cannot skimp here. Get the best trainers and pay them well, as they will influence your business. Get involved and play an active role. Show your commitment to the process, the training team, and the overall organization. When times are tough, invest more heavily in training and resist the urge to pull back. Done right, training will make a significant and long-lasting difference in your business.

CHAPTER 22

BEST PRACTICES

"If it's being done, it can be done," is one of my all-time favorite professional sayings. It is a confirmation for me. This builds confidence that we can hire well and that we can have stretch goals that allow for top performers to elevate their performances to the expected level and beyond. Identifying your best people is a major lever in your organization. Once you identify the best people, you can dissect what they do, build a training plan mirroring their actions and approach, and train the balance of your staff. First, you have to identify those people and look at the "who," the "what," and the "how":

- Who is consistently surpassing goals?
- What is driving them to achieve at these consistent levels?
- How are they doing it?

The key is to identify these people, ensuring that you have taken into consideration any factors that may enfranchise them. In other words, are they in a territory that is much more rewarding than some others? Do they have a client base that thinks, looks, or acts differently? In order to have credibility about a best practice approach, you must ensure that you truly have an apples-to-apples comparison in which all things are reasonably equal and some people are simply achieving at a much higher level than others.

How often have you had a supervisor who starts a sentence with the phrase "When I used to..."? The outcome rarely has much impact and is likely highly irrelevant. It may also cause the occasional eye roll. Relevance comes when we put like situations together. "When I used to..." looks at things as they were done in the past, which is likely quite irrelevant for the person failing today. Best practices allow for us to look at people doing the exact same job at the exact same time in a bit of a different way in which the magic can be dissected, understood, bottled, and shared. Used correctly, best practice sharing will alter the trajectory of your business.

There are three distinct types of best practice sharing. By employing all three, you can allow many more people to be viewed as experts, thus allowing for personal confidence to grow and the organization's culture to flourish. If you simply look at the top person and try to dissect everything that he or she does, resentment can develop toward him or her, and the result will lack the overall impact on the organization. Let's focus on the three areas:

- **General best practice sharing**—This looks at the top people within a peer group, based solely on overall success against goals. This can be powerful, especially with a distributed team. If you are utilizing rankings, everyone wants to know what the best people are doing that keeps them at the top of the charts.

- **Geographic best practice sharing**—The truth is that there are regional differences. If you solely identify people who do well in New York City, those in Dallas, Los Angeles, or Seattle will find marginal credibility in the process, as their client base likely behaves differently. By looking for best practices within given geographic areas, you will heighten the credibility of your program.

- **KPI best practice sharing**—If you are measuring various key performance indicators, it is important to recognize those performing highly within each. In other words, one rep may be great at limiting refunds, while another may be great at increasing the client base. Both aspects are critical to the success of your business. Identify those who excel at specific KPIs, and dissect their steps to success.

Now that we have identified the top performers, based on overall, geographic, and KPI performance, where do we go from here? Start by engaging the training team. Let them know about the initiative, outlining the significance of the undertaking, and that they will be responsible for putting together content. Then, as the leader, reach out to each best practice employee personally. Congratulate them and let them know about the initiative. They will be excited on two fronts. First, they will be excited that you reached out to them and recognized them for their achievements. Second, they will take pride that they are being viewed as leaders among their peers. This is a powerful secondary benefit of best practice sharing.

In order to truly understand the "how" behind the best practice team's success, you will need to identify and understand the way the team members go about their work. I have been intimately involved in best practice initiatives for the better part of my thirty years of leadership. After all of those years and after studying hundreds of top reps, I will go on record as stating that there is no silver bullet. Top performers come in all shapes and sizes. They are men and women, single and married, parents and grandparents. For the most part, they don't use charm or some hard-to-replicate tactic. They simply do the blocking and tackling better, more consistently, and more often than others. Every time I go through this exercise, it reaffirms the fact that we have a process that works and that we can teach to others. It is not about personality. It is about following the process. It all comes down to saying the right things and saying them enough times. At the end of the day, it's all about execution.

So how do we leverage our best people to bring success to this initiative? Here are several ideas:

- **Use the best practice team to assist in building your script**—There is nobody better in the organization to help build the talk track than those performing at the highest levels.
- **Use the best practice team to present to the new-hire class**—Again, leveraging those actually doing, rather than those training, has much more impact. Bring them in for ten- or fifteen-minute chats with the class throughout the week. Prior to them presenting, set them up by introducing them as the best in the given area of discussion. Ensure that the best practice team

is fully aligned with the standards, scripting, values and expectations of the company. There must be complete alignment here, or the process will break down.

- **Use the best practice team as the comparison set for recruitment**—Earlier, we discussed this tactic when employing personality profiling. It is imperative that you bounce a candidate's profile against a comparison set made up of your best practice performers.

- **Use an online video tool to interview your best people**—Ask them ten questions, and make the video fun. Set up a weekly best practice–sharing program, in which you send out a video on the same day every week, so people anticipate it coming on that day. Kicking off with a positive learning experience ensures an enlightening start to the day. Once the team members have viewed the video, your managers then can ask them what they learned and how they intend to apply those learnings. Watching the video is just part of the skill-transfer process.

- **Record the screen for video and audio content capture**—If you have a team that primarily works in an inside role with client contact via computer, there is software available that allows you to capture the call and watch the process the rep goes through on his or her screen. In some businesses, reps have ten or more screens and ten or more reference documents open at a time. This software will help you see which documents and screens are actually important and applicable. The recording can be used for internal training and real-world best practice sharing.

Your people are your most important asset. Your best people are your most important training asset. Identify the best. Uncover what motivates them. Dissect exactly what they do, and then train others in those tactics and processes. There is no better training than tapping into the expertise of your best people. Everyone wins in that process.

CHAPTER 23

COMPENSATION

"You get what you pay for" is a common saying when comparing products and services. How comfortable would you be in hiring a contractor who would reroof your home for half of what others charge? Would you be willing to pay top dollar for a signed collectible that didn't have a letter of authenticity? Risky, right? We are faced with these types of choices every day, and depending on the situation and the importance of the need, we will make a choice between price and quality. Seldom do we get both in a product/service decision. Very often, there is a direct correlation between price and quality. As the old saying goes, "The bitterness of poor quality remains long after the sweetness of low price is forgotten."

While the premise of "You get what you pay for" certainly holds true for recruiting talent, my intention is to tackle this phrase in a different way in this chapter. As we broach the subject of compensation, I'd like to present the idea that you will get the *result* that you are willing to pay for. Said differently, people will do what you are willing to pay them to do.

Building effective compensation plans begins with a very clear understanding of what we are intending to achieve. We have to be laser focused on the goals of the organization before we can craft a compensation plan that will lead us to the intended target. Once we understand the goal, we can determine the levers that need to be pulled in order to achieve the outcome we seek. Those levers then become the areas that determine the components of our compensation plan. We will drive our KPIs if we focus on and compensate for them. The key is to align the KPIs to the goal and grade/compensate at every level throughout the channel (front line, management, executive). Consistent alignment to the goal through the organization is key.

In developing an effective compensation plan, consider the following:

- **View compensation in its entirety**—Building a comp plan based heavily on the base salary is a mistake. While base salary is an important component, compensation must be developed based on a commitment to all components: base salary, variable compensation, benefits, 401(k), equity, etc.
- **Test the waters**—Before rolling out a plan, form a compensation committee made up of a strong cross section of talent. Bring general ideas forward in the first meeting and elicit feedback. In subsequent meetings, share specifics and gain buy-in. Those affected by variable comp plans are rarely those involved in the development of variable comp plans. This is a perfect example of ownership through authorship. When people have their hands in the development,

they will support the result outwardly among their peers.

- **Monitor the market**—When we have a buyer's market in which the candidate has the leverage, base salary will play an increasingly important role. When we have a seller's market in which companies have leverage in negotiations, we can have a more equitable balance between base and variable pay. In either scenario, you don't have to offer the highest base salary. Rather, it is important that you are competitive in base salary and your overall comp package is strong. While a deviation could cause internal disruption if existing employees catch wind of the adjustment, we must compete for talent given the current environment. If that means adjusting current existing employees also, then do it.

- **KISS**—Keep it simple, stupid. Employees need to understand exactly how they are being paid. If a variable plan is part of your strategy, which it should be, the goal is to make it so simple that a rep can come out of a sales call and know exactly how much he or she made on that close. This will prove to be a great motivator.

- **It's all about effective goal setting**—A strong comp plan coupled with poor goal setting will lead to epic failure and a level of distrust toward the company. The only way the comp plan accomplishes the goal is if employees see the goal as a stretch but still attainable. If the goal seems unreachable, the reps will view overdelivery earnings opportunities as unreachable as well, and overdelivery accelerators are what keep your A players in your company. Get the goals right. Stretch them, but don't break them.

- **99 percent is failure**—In setting effective goals, people must understand the definition of success. If a variable compensation cut in point is at 70 percent of achievement, without proper definition, a person may equate receiving commissions with success. Therefore, we must be diligent in our definition of success. While we may choose to compensate at achievement levels below 100 percent, we must be clear that overall achievement below 100 percent is considered failure. Now, I know this sounds harsh, but if goals have been set to be "stretch but attainable," how can we applaud achievement below 100 percent? The goal is the expectation and the "keep your job" number. Our teams must be aware that falling short of the goal too often will lead to being employed elsewhere. Harsh or not, we are here to support the initiatives of a growing organization and to maintain employment for all non-quota-bearing employees. Those with quotas have a job to do, and they are graded on their ability to deliver beyond the 100 percent expectation threshold.

- **Resist adjusting the plan too often**—Adjusting goals monthly or quarterly (depending on your business) is acceptable and expected, as seasonality plays a role in the decision process. That said, stay away from adjusting the components of the compensation plan. Take time up front to ensure alignment with company goals and agreed-to KPIs. If you have these pieces right, there is no need to adjust the core components of the plan.

- **Start with** *why*—Communicating the variable comp plan transparently and openly is critical to the success of the program and the acceptance of those who will be affected by variable comp. In rolling out the plan, start with *why*. Explain why you do what you do, the strategic vision, the goals of the organization, and the KPIs that will determine success. When you start with *why*, the plan will flow from that conversation. When you openly share the overarching goals, you then slide into the KPIs that will achieve those goals. When people understand the needs of their clients and their business, they will readily accept their role in delivering on the KPIs that will influence the outcomes.

- **Provide examples**—When rolling out the variable plan, show examples of levels of performance on both the old plan and the new one. Be very open about the commitment to overdelivery. After viewing examples, those affected will clearly see the commitment to winning and the willingness to pay for success.

- **There is a greater need**—When rolling out the variable comp plan, remind those on the front line that their efforts and results fuel the entire organization and the families of those behind the scenes. Help them understand that it is not about them, but about the entire employee base and their families. When people understand the impact they have on the lives of others beyond their clients, you create an environment of outward thinkers. A company of outward thinkers leads to an enviable culture.

- **Hold ground**—If there are questions about the variable comp plan (and there will be), always ask two questions: "What would you do differently?" and "How does what you are suggesting best suit the needs of the company and your clients?" This exercise goes a long way toward eliminating "me" thinking.

- **"Reverse Robin Hood"**—In business, our goal is to create a level playing field so that everyone can flourish. In developing a variable compensation plan, our goal is to reward those who excel, keeping them happy, enthused, passionate, driven, and in our employ. This principle recommends that we steal from the poor and give to the rich—hence, "Reverse Robin Hood." (Robin Hood stole from the rich and gave to the poor.) The truth is that we have developed a target-variable comp model that is baked into the budget. As a leadership team, our job is to determine how we appropriate those dollars. Assuming that we provide an equal opportunity to succeed, consistent tools, and training, I have little sympathy for poor performers. In fact, I would recommend setting a level in which falling below that designated marker, would dictate an employee earning no commissions or bonus, over that compensation period. Take the money that would have gone to those performing at a subpar level and shift it to the overdelivery side of the equation. Those who underdeliver will self-select out in time, affording you an opportunity to topgrade with little extra effort. Those who overdeliver will be motivated and driven to excel, month in and month out. Overpay for performance.
- **Build hefty accelerators**—Ramp your payout percentages heavily once a person surpasses his or her

target. Build in escalators at key levels (110 percent, 120 percent, 150 percent, 200 percent, etc.). At each plateau, percent payouts accelerate greatly. This will keep top players wanting to drive to the next level.

- **Focus on activities rather than results**—Once goals and compensation have been established, clearly articulating the activities that will lead to those results must take center stage. Staring at a big number can be intimidating. Effective leadership calls for working backward from the goal by looking at the end result in bite-size chunks. In other words, break the goals down by month, week, and day, but more importantly, identify the activities that will lead to the result you seek. By understanding the average deal/order size as well as the close rate (how many calls lead to appointments and how many appointments lead to a close), you can then focus on the least common denominators: calls and appointments. When you focus on activities, success is within your control. It becomes less about the number and more about controlling actions.

- **Get everyone aligned**—The only way the whole variable compensation process works is if salespeople, sales managers, vice presidents of sales, and chief sales officers are aligned to, accountable for, and compensated on the same goals within the same periods of time. If a 20 percent conversion rate is a key marker for the business, then everyone should have that as a KPI and a component of their compensation plan. Comp plans break down when there is misalignment within given channels. If managers are compensated on different KPIs than their employees, then there is misalignment.

- **Pay managers on the percentage of their players who succeed**—This is the one exception to getting everyone aligned. While managers should have the same KPIs as their direct reports, they should have one additional component. Countless times, I have seen managers surpass their goals, while only a small percentage of their direct reports achieve theirs. One high flyer can take a team to great heights. In order to lessen this impact, compensate your managers based on the percentage of their direct reports who hit their goals within the given period. If less than 50 percent achieve their goals, the manager gets zero dollars in bonuses on that component. When a manager has 80 percent of his or her direct reports over goal, pay him or her a boatload. Great leaders know whom they serve and serve them with great vigor and passion. For a leader, surpassing goal is about both individual and team achievements. Goal achievement is hollow unless the full team does it together. Again, you will get what you pay for. Pay leaders well to focus on the success of every one of their direct reports, and they will achieve. When people feel commitment from their managers, and they win, they won't leave. Help your managers to help their people. Pay them, and they will.

- **Tie trainers to new-hire success**—Trainers should be tied to the success of the trainees with whom they work. With new-hire trainers, their variable comp should be tied directly to the success of those whom they serve: the new hires. Set ramp goals for the new hires, and make that roll-up goal the goal for the trainer during a predetermined period (three to six months). I would also highly recommend that the trainers have a component on the percentage of new hires who achieve their goals, as has also been recommended for managers.

- **Build comp calculators**—Comp calculators allow people to plug in numbers and see what their payouts will look like. Top performers love this tool. Have the managers incorporate this into weekly meetings with their respective direct reports. This is a big motivator. Keep the compensation opportunity front and center while aligning it to the goals of the individual. Determine what he or she is working toward—a house, a car, etc.

- **Clearly communicate results**—Companies have a tendency to fall down here by neglecting to send out commission statements and asking their people to trust them. When it comes to money, there is no trust, only full and timely transparency. Make it a priority to send commission statements out to all employees within seven days of the close of the compensation period. The manager should be the person to share the good news first. Managers need to tell their people about their commissions and go through the statements with them, recognizing and reinforcing a job well done.

- **Never mess with a person's money**—You cannot— and I repeat cannot—make mistakes on commissions and bonuses. You can make mistakes in a lot of areas, but this and recruitment are places where you cannot misstep. This is about trust, respect, and responsibility. Get it right, and get it on time.

People work for a multitude of different reasons, but compensation will always be at or near the top of the priority list. We are in a war for talent. Make no mistake about it. People will go where they are valued and paid for their efforts. Building an effective compensation model will play a big role in your ability to attract and maintain talent. Make a commitment to developing a compensation plan that is highly competitive, easy to understand, and filled with opportunity for top performers to earn well beyond target. Well beyond. Overpay your top performers, and they will never leave you.

CHAPTER 24

SEGMENTATION AND ALIGNMENT

In several previous chapters, I have driven home the point about the *why* behind your business and why you do what you do in the way that you do it. There is nothing more important to your clients and more rewarding to your employees than the reason your company exists—your *why*. When we discuss processes, we turn to the mechanics of the business and shift our focus to *who* and *how*.

In determining our approach in bringing our product/ service to the market, we must understand our target audience (*who*), segment our approach, and align employee skill sets to the goals of our business and the needs of our clients (*how*).

Often, I see businesses approach their target audiences in consistent ways, with consistent messages, regardless of business need or business type. While consistent messaging is critical, it must be tailored to accommodate the channel or client type. For example, imagine selling advertising to large national brands in the same way that you would approach a small mom-and-pop shop. The clients' needs are different, so the approach and language must be different as well. What is important to a small business operator is different than what is important to an enterprise-level organization. Segmentation is necessary in order to approach groups of similar people in a way that they expect to be approached, in a language that is understandable to them, and by people who understand their unique buying behaviors. The appropriate approach will be determined by the complexity of the offering and the defined segments. There are many ways to tailor your sales approach:

- **Vertical segmentation**—If you have a business that serves a broad array of industries, breaking your contact approach vertically is a beneficial approach. This allows for you to align your internal resources to become expert within that given industry. For example, if one of your key/core target industries is healthcare, you could build a vertical approach, complete with vertical-specific materials and deep training on classifications such as sports and fitness, hospitals, dentists, physicians, senior services, etc., with subclassification training that would go a level deeper. The goal is to develop an approach that allows your team to understand the vertical in a deep and profound way, so that when they approach the client/prospect, credibility comes as a result.
- **Geographic segmentation**—By segmenting geographically, you can align employees to clients based on location. There are multiple benefits to this strategy. First, depending on your offering, utilizing a geographic approach can provide a sense of hyperlocal

alignment. In other words, a client would be speaking with someone who knows his or her area and the unique differences within that specific territory. Second, there is a three-hour time difference between the East and West Coasts of the United States, causing challenges if your team resides in Los Angeles but a sizable set of your clients resides in Boston. Segmenting geographically has clear advantages.

- **Prospect/client segmentation**—Also known as a "hunter/farmer" approach, this allows for different approaches based on whether a segment includes existing clients or target prospects. The approaches and messaging are vastly different, requiring employees with different skill sets and different sets of KPIs.

- **Prospect/client size segmentation**—Approaching very large firms adds complexity to the buying process. Having a team equipped to maneuver around these complexities has definite advantages.

- **Client spend segmentation**—Segmenting by spend is an important approach. Key accounts likely have different needs than prospects or low-spend clients. Implemented properly, special treatment of key clients (rewards programs, awards, etc.) drives allegiance and helps to defend against competitive threats.

- **Lapsed client segmentation**—Past clients are often overlooked as a solid segment yet provide a great opportunity for reengagement.

- **Product/service segmentation**—This can be tricky, as having multiple touches within the same organization could result in confusion, but there are times where having specific product/service knowledge is a solid approach. This works especially well when the products are highly specialized and complex.

In regard to segmentation, there is no right or wrong way, and rarely is there one approach utilized. Depending on your offering, multiple approaches are warranted. Test different strategies and settle in on those that align best with your clients, employees, and overall business. Segmentation is necessary. It's simply a matter of finding the approaches that best fit your demographic, geographic, and overall client needs.

Now that we have determined the approach, it is time to determine the alignment, as there are two sides to this equation: client-dictated needs and employee-determined skill sets. In determining which people call on which clients, consider the following:

- **Experience**—This is where resumes come in handy. Look at your sales folks and examine their levels of experience in outbound roles. Were they primarily focused on clients or prospects and most importantly, how did they fare in those roles? Find people who have sales experience and success in their backgrounds. Whether in a hunter or a farmer role, selling is core of success. Avoid self-proclaimed account managers, as they may view *sales* as a dirty word. We all sell, whether in a frontline account management or a pure sales role.
- **Aptitude**—Depending on the complexity of your offering, the devil may be in the details. Find people

147

who align with the needs of the segment. If there is a high level of sophistication necessary in targeting clients based on a particular vertical, ensure that the employee's skill sets align. If stellar written and oral communication is critical to a role, ensure that the chosen employee is credible in his or her written and verbal skills. Test prior to rolling. Nothing kills credibility more quickly than poor grammar or a poor approach.

- **Attitude**—In a highly strategic sales environment, avoid placing employees who possess a fast-paced and high-volume mind-set in this role, and vice versa. In many instances, I have worked with people who possess the skills necessary to work in both a hunting and a farming role. That said, I recall an equal number of people who would fail in one or the other. For the most part, there is a mind-set difference between hunters and farmers and enterprise-level salespeople versus those focused on selling to small businesses.

- **Geography**—Whenever possible, place people in a geographical location near their homes or offices. For both clients and employees, familiarity breeds confidence. As discussed previously, style awareness is an important feature in determining successful outcomes. Placing a high-intensity person in a low-intensity location will lead to failure.

Determining your client/prospect approach is a key factor in determining success. Knowing your audience and segmenting it based on need, personality, demographic, engagement, usage, and geography, as well as aligning your internal talent to those differentiating factors, will allow for an approach that will ensure optimal engagement and success.

CHAPTER 25

STANDARDS AND ACCOUNTABILITY

A standard is a level of quality, achievement, etc., that is considered acceptable or desirable. In other words, standards are minimally acceptable benchmarks. Taking it one step further, standards are what you are willing to accept. In order for standards to be understood and adhered to, they must first be clearly defined and openly communicated. In order for standards to be embraced, there must be a clear understanding of the *why* behind them, or they will simply be viewed as rules—and nobody likes rules. Standards are the pieces that make up the puzzle. They are the components that lead to the goal. When done right and consistently practiced, goals are within reach. Standards are what we stand for and what we believe should be the way we approach our business. It is the way we present ourselves internally and externally. Standards must be clearly defined and consistently applied.

Standards fall into four distinct categories: communication standards, activity standards, delivery standards, and values standards. Here are a few ideas that may be worthy of implementation:

- **Communication standards**—How we expect our team members to engage with internal and external clients.

    o *Responsiveness*—Set a standard expectation for response timing, whether to a coworker or a client. We will be judged based on our ability to respond quickly to the needs of clients. In a hypercompetitive situation and in our culture of immediate gratification, response time is often the difference between getting business and losing business. Be aggressive here. In today's world of technology, we are all tethered and have the ability to respond quickly. With every interaction, there is an opportunity to be judged by our clients. Often commitment is tied directly to speed of response.

    o *Talk track*—We've discussed the need to follow a script or talk track. Proper messaging can often make the difference between success and failure, in your results and in your brand. Whether it be your elevator pitch, an e-mail to a client, or a full-fledged presentation on capabilities, consistency of messaging is critical. Leave little to chance. Map out your talk track, and ensure that everyone practices messaging consistently.

    o *Daily one-on-ones*—Over my career, I have used daily "seven-minute meetings" in addressing the need to briefly touch base with each of my employees in the morning. Back in my early career, when I was leading frontline teams, we would have seven-minute meetings first thing every morning. Whether in person or over the phone, these meetings would allow me to get a feel for each of my employees' plans for the day and to ensure that they had positive mind-sets in approaching the day. Sales can be a lonely profession, complete with lots of rejection every day. Having a positive conversation prior to hitting the streets often leads to an uplifted spirit and a strong focus for the day ahead. The key is to keep the meetings deliberately brief, sharing a story or a finding from another employee. Your goal is to provide a good nugget for your employee to take forward that day. This is less of a checkup and more of a pump up, letting your employee know that you are there to support him or her in every way possible. Commit to these daily. It's easy to find a reason to cancel them. Effective leaders make these interactions a priority and as a result build confident and deep relationships with their people.

o *Success sharing*—As mentioned previously, it can be very lonely in the field every day, facing rejection and avoidance. When a person is having a bad day, he or she has a tendency to believe that his or her peers are equally challenged. Get in the habit of sharing successes twice per day, once in the morning and once in the afternoon. Whether through group texts or chats, sharing good news will have a positive impact on those who may be struggling. Again, positivity builds momentum and spirit. The more you commit to sharing good news, the better the momentum you will build, the culture you will create, and the results you will achieve.

o *Nightly updates*—These are effective and necessary communication tools when you are involved in a fast-paced, high-volume, monthly goal business. When you have thirty days to achieve your goal, you cannot afford to go days without communicating status. Pacing plays a key role, with daily consistency being a key marker. Nightly updates allow recognition of those pacing well and are a reminder to all of where they should be at a given point in the month. In a monthly goal business, creating a sense of urgency on day one is more important than creating urgency on day thirty-one. Creating a fun, nightly update communication keeps the urgency high and the team focused on the principle of tackling their goals in "bite-size" chunks.

o *Weekly team newsletters*—Create a team name and have a theme for the month. Put a fun weekly newsletter together, sharing successes for the week and recognizing those who are leading the way and doing a great job.

o *Monday morning team calls*—There's nothing better than kicking off a week with a team call. Bring guests on the call to share things happening within the company. Have one or two team members share a best practice or success from the previous week. Recognize great performances and set a goal for the upcoming week.

Share company news. This call takes preparation in order to bring value. Avoid having meetings to simply have meetings. Focus on bringing real value.

o *Monthly/quarterly recognition calls*—Share successes, best practices, and results. Recognize achievement.

- **Activity standards**—These are the actions that we expect our team members to take throughout a given day.

  o *CRM diligence*—Every day, expect your team members to update their CRM (customer relationship management) tool. Help them understand that we are all about helping our clients, and the CRM allows us to understand our client interactions and needs. Accurate information also leads to understanding our business needs most appropriately. We can't manage what we can't measure; thus, the input is critical for our future direction as an organization. I'd go as far as stating that updating the CRM daily is a condition of employment.

  o *Activity reports*—By focusing on actions, we influence outcomes. Focusing on the quota gets us nowhere aside from creating self-inflicted stress. Understanding the daily actions that lead to our achieving the end goal is how the true magic comes together. Build an alert through your CRM that is delivered to each leader every morning. These alerts will outline the number of appointments scheduled, for that day and the next, for each salesperson. If we truly believe that our actions influence our outcomes and that each day makes up a bite-size chunk of the desired result, then why would we not ensure that the proper actions are set for today and tomorrow? The goal of the daily activity report is to ensure flow and avoid end-of-month, end-of-quarter, or deadline stress. By committing to a consistent level of activity every day, we control our fate, and we avoid the stress that is often associated with a close or a deadline. This is not intended to be a "checker upper," but rather a "helper outer." With stress comes a difference in our tone, our approach, our talk track, and our decision making. By treating each day equally, we focus on flow, we maintain consistency in our approach, and we eliminate stress.

o *Field time*—Very few activities with real impact occur behind a desk. Leaders need to be in the field with their people. Set daily/weekly field time expectations for leaders. This allows for consistent activity and a culture of teamwork, allowing for a lessening of any *us versus them* thinking. Great things happen in the field. Connections are formed, bonds are strengthened, ideas are generated, and client needs are best understood.

- **Delivery standards**—These include the results that we expect our team members to achieve:
  o *Pacing*—In a time-bound, deadline-driven environment, hitting benchmarks and maintaining a

consistent flow of work is imperative. Salespeople often pace slowly over the first half of the month or quarter and then attempt to close the gap over the second half of the month or quarter. As leaders, we must set benchmarks in order to set an even tone and avoid the stress that accompanies deadlines. We must emphasize the need to perform consistently, day in and day out, and to avoid peaks and valleys. Set benchmarks, and communicate them daily/weekly, sharing where members of the team need to be, individually and collectively, at each point along the continuum. Visibility and accountability are critical in order to ensure adherence.

o *Goal achievement*—As discussed previously, the only acceptable standard within a success-driven environment is goal-plus achievement. The team must be aware that a goal is the minimal acceptable level in your organization.

o *PIP implementation*—If people miss their goals consistently, they must understand that there is a consequence to that failure. Clearly define the performance improvement plans (PIP) that are a part of the accountability value of the organization and explain that the ultimate goal is, as the name suggests, improvement. People will miss goals. Define the time line or lack of successful consistency that will result in a PIP. If you are in a monthly quota business, back-to-back monthly misses could result in going on to a plan for the next month.

If a person misses three months in a row, he or she would be terminated. If you happen to be in a quarterly quota–driven business, you would determine if missing in a quarter would warrant a PIP for the following quarter. These are decisions that only you can make. The key is to define success and the consequences that come as a result of missing. If you truly seek a performance-driven culture, this must be a part of that culture. Expectations without consequences for underdelivery lead to complacency and a clear lack of urgency.

In a success-driven culture, there need to be clearly defined and openly shared measures. KPIs must be understood, and achievement must be recognized. One way of accomplishing this is through a ranking system. There are two schools of thought about ranking employees. Those against ranking feel that it creates a pressure-filled environment and a culture that can lead to negativity. Those in favor of a ranked system believe that it brings visibility to the key components of the business, recognizes those who perform well, and brings light to those lacking in certain areas critical to the success of the business. I am a firm believer that top performers are driven by knowing where they stand and that a culture lacking visibility also lacks accountability. If we embrace the mission, we must also embrace the components that lead to our succeeding at that mission. Those components are our KPIs. These are the pieces that will determine our success and, ultimately, our fate. To hide our success or failure in the progress toward our KPIs would deprive the team of the full transparency that we have embraced as a core value of our organization.

Here are the components that make up a solid ranking system:

- **Choose seven to ten KPIs that are critical to your business**—Determine those criteria and ensure that everyone is aware of the importance of each of them. Define them directly on the ranking itself.
- **Rank each category**—If there are twenty people being ranked, the highest performer will receive a number one rank in that category. The next-best performer in that category would receive a number two rank, and so on.
- **Place weightings on each KPI**—While all of the defined KPIs are important, some hold more importance than others. The most important KPIs should hold 2.0 weight. The next-most important should have 1.0 weight. Those less important should hold 0.5 weight. This will ultimately lead to the best ranking. For example, a person receiving a rank of three in a 2.0 weighted category would receive six total points in that category.
- **Tabulate the total points**—Add the tabulated points across the row to determine the total points for each employee.
- **Rank from lowest points to highest points**—The rep with the lowest points total has consistently ranked the best within the collection of categories.
- **Color-code each ranked column**—Highlight in green those who are in the top one-third of each category.

The middle one-third will be in white, and the bottom one-third will be in red. This will provide a strong visual on how each person is performing as compared to his or her peers in each category.

- **Calculate peer averages**—At the bottom of each column, calculate the average score for all ranked employees. This will provide a view into how each person is performing versus the group as a whole.

Here is an abbreviated version of a simple ranking:

Weight	2.0		1.0		1.0		1.0		0.5	
Rep	YTD % Goal Attainment	Rank	YTD Conversion %	Rank	YTD Average $ Sale	Rank	YTD # New Clients	Rank	YTD % Refunds	Rank	Total Points
Diane	110%	2	48%	2	$1,000	1	125	1	22%	6	11
Alyssa	108%	3	49%	1	$775	2	119	2	14%	2	12
Carly	112%	1	45%	3	$680	3	112	3	17%	4	13
Gary	99%	4	38%	5	$555	7	65	5	8%	1	25.5
Bill	88%	6	34%	7	$625	5	82	4	16%	3	29.5
Joe	92%	5	36%	6	$645	4	48	6	26%	5	28.5
Brian	76%	7	42%	4	$575	6	44	7	28%	7	34.5
Average	98%		42%		$694		85		19%		

In this example, there are the makings of a good conversation with each employee. Here are a few examples:

- **Diane**—In four of the five categories, Diane does really well, ranking first or second in each of them. She is also well ahead of goal. Lots of kudos to go around. That said, there is an area of opportunity in refunds for Diane. As her leader, I would work closely with her on improvement here or have her work with Gary, who ranks first in that category and who can cross-train and assist in her further development.
- **Alyssa**—She is strong across the board, ranking in the top three in every category. I see her as a potential

top performer and will work to light a fire to get her to the top position.

- **Carly**—As the top performer in the most important category (percentage of goal attainment, 2.0 weight), she is strong. In several categories, she is slightly above average. With effective coaching, I could move her up the ranks.

- **Brian**—This is likely a more difficult yet necessary conversation. Brian ranks dead last in three categories, including percentage of goal. He is also below his peer average in five of the six categories. By having a ranking, not only do I have a platform for a discussion but Brian can also clearly see that he is underperforming in quite a few areas that are critical to his success and the success of our organization. By publishing a weekly ranking, I can chart his progress and development. If the will is there and improvement is noted, I will work with him. If progress is slight or nonexistent, I will place Brian on a PIP and likely look to displace him unless he shows substantial progress. This also triggers the need to begin recruitment processes to backfill. While I want to be fair, I can't be too patient here. Ranking last in multiple categories illustrates a lack of will, skill, or both. I will need to move swiftly and decisively.

Ranking brings light to the key success factors of an organization. With it, you can identify areas of opportunity for your team members and influence the trajectory of their respective careers. Without this level of visibility, you would be flying blind, managing people based on gut feelings and subjectivity. Managing by gut will not move the needle. Managing by metrics will.

Along with a standard weekly ranking, rank your team members on initiatives or individual products. Again, with heat and light come commitment and growth.

CHAPTER 26

SALES ENABLEMENT, EFFICIENCY, AND PRIORITIZATION

The most successful organizations understand the importance of having a powerful frontline sales team, but they also realize that success contribution extends well beyond the sales organization. Successful companies leverage the talents and expertise of complementary and support teams to influence revenue-driving efforts. While the sales organization has the distinct advantage (or disadvantage) of transparency and visibility, it is through the commitment and efforts of other divisions that long-lasting and significant impact on the overall success of the organization is felt. Credit is due far beyond the frontline sales team.

Sales enablement, also known as sales operations, plays a very important role within an organization. The purpose of the sales enablement division, in its simplest form, is to develop a process that equips the sales team with the proper approach, tools, systems, and deployment strategies to maximize efficiency and execution.

As we discussed in chapter 21, investing in a division that cannot directly contribute to the revenue outcome can be a tough pill for some to swallow. It takes near-term and long-term commitment at all levels, in good times and bad, to venture down this path. The company will feel the benefits. The key is to clearly articulate the role, the responsibilities, and the projected impact of this division while putting measures in place to articulate the effect the team is having on the organization as a whole.

The investment necessary is tied directly to the size of the organization, requiring further commitment to scale as the organization scales. Identifying and understanding the proper support-to-sales ratio will be an important task throughout the implementation and justification process. In order to find success in the enablement division, you must recruit a leader with deep experience in the areas of compensation administration/design, deployment, segmentation, analytics/reporting, collateral development, product implementation, and project management. The scope of the enablement division's responsibilities is open to debate, as is the reporting hierarchy. My recommendation would be for enablement to report directly to the head of sales. Depending on the abilities and experience of the head of sales, certain responsibilities may align directly with him or her versus one level removed to the operations/enablement leader. The role of the head of sales, as well as that of the operations leader, will need to be well defined. Here is a view of the many roles and responsibilities that could be aligned with the enablement leader:

- **Compensation design and administration**—Enablement will be responsible for architecting a compensation plan that will align with organizational goals and drive performance. The team will also be responsible for distributing commission statements and administering the plan. The team will work closely with finance and sales to ensure proper design and implementation.

- **Segmentation**—The team will bring forward ideas on how to optimize the client approach, based on its findings and client/employee/leadership feedback. This will include determining the most profitable target audience as well as full territory design. This area will require determinations of optimal head count and workforce management, as well as the defining of the responsibilities of each role. Time-in-motion studies need to be understood in order to best influence opportunities for greater efficiency and prioritize automation needs appropriately.

- **Product implementation**—Team members will work closely with marketing, product, and sales to determine further product needs and rollout plans. They will also work closely with training to facilitate communication and implementation.

- **Pricing**—The team will study pricing and the competitive landscape while working with sales/marketing and visiting clients to determine ways to simplify and optimize pricing.

- **Competitive analysis**—The team will stay abreast of competitive advantages and advances and develop tools to best understand how to present propositions in the most advantageous ways.

- **Analytics**—In place of, or in advance of, a full analytics team, the enablement team will be responsible for cohort and churn analysis for both clients and employees.

- **CRM administration**—The enablement team will be responsible for CRM updates and reporting, ensuring that timely and accurate reports are sent out to all necessary parties. In addition, this team will be responsible for developing reports to bring full transparency and visibility to the business. They will also administer all weekly rankings.

- **Sales collateral**—The team will be responsible for sales tools and materials for internal use and external exposure. Team members will work closely with sales and marketing to ensure needs are being met, both proactively and reactively.

- **Training**—Depending on the skills, experience, and wishes of the head of sales, training responsibility may fall under enablement, or the training team may report separately and directly to the head of sales. Training is a very important responsibility, and unless the enablement leader has had direct and effective experience leading training, the responsibility for training would best be served by reporting into the head of sales. This would include all best practice sharing as well.

- **Prioritization**—The enablement leader will need to have the ability to prioritize tasks. Looking at each request and responsibility individually, he or she must be able to determine priorities based the potential impact and projected return on investment of each request. If everything is a priority, nothing is a priority. The leader must be able to synthesize findings and prioritize opportunities based on the ultimate potential reward to the organization.

So how do we determine the impact that the enablement division is having on the overall organization? As the sales enablement team is an "expense" division, the key will be to bring objective measures to the forefront of the discussion while also tying compensation to organizational KPIs. We all own success together, and the more closely that we can tie enablement compensation to organizational goals, the more the enablement division will look like a direct extension of the sales channel. This will also place accountability front and center for the members of the enablement team. They will understand that their compensation is tied to the success of the organization, creating an urgency to influence outcomes and implement needs swiftly, accurately, and passionately. Here are a few potential accountability measures:

- **Conversion rates**—A consistent KPI for most organizations is in the area of conversion rates. Simply put, conversion rates are calculated by determining the number of clients, versus the universe of prospects, who take the specific actions you want them to. By providing simplified, competitive pricing, strong collateral/messaging, aligned deployment, sophisticated direction based on analytics, and highly visible reporting, conversion rates will undoubtedly be affected. If conversion rates are measured and compensation is based on those measurements, the enablement team will be accountable for delivering on its key initiatives in a timely and highly effective way.

- **Mean lift**—By determining the average, or mean, we have a starting point for goal setting. Determine the lift you seek by KPI, and tie the enablement team to that figure. As one measure will likely include either gross or net revenues, this will align quite well with the executive team's compensation marker. Again, I would recommend this as a piece of the compensation model, not the full model. The more tightly that you can align direct impact to compensation, the better. Determining multiple KPIs, rather than solely a top-line or bottom-line revenue number, would be most beneficial.
- **New-hire ramp**—If training is aligned with enablement, improvement in new-hire ramp is a solid criterion for measurement.

Making a commitment to sales enablement will allow the organization to study the inner workings of the company and assist in perfecting the components that greatly influence the path to success. These fundamentals are the building blocks of success and need committed attention and prioritization.

CHAPTER 27

COMMUNICATION

Throughout this book, we have emphasized the importance of open, honest, consistent, and transparent communication. Nothing is more vital to the health of the organization and the trust of the team than engaging dialogue. Employees want to be intimately involved and to understand how their values align with the values of the organization. Employees want to feel that their contributions are making a difference. With effective communication, we break down walls, eliminate barriers, build trust, and create a culture of oneness. When a leader fosters a team-driven and inclusive culture, amazing things follow. As an affirmation, here are several keys to effective communication:

- **Be authentic**—Be yourself. Be honest. Be vulnerable. Don't try to be who you think people want to you to be. They will see through that. Be authentically "you." There is risk in being authentic, but the rewards trump all risk. This is a no-compromise area.

People will respect you for letting your true and personal self shine through brightly.

- **Be genuine**—Lead with your heart. This allows others to view your honesty and sincerity and affords them the opportunity to do the same. Being genuine is about warmth and says a lot about you as a human. This is your feeling side. Share it openly, and you will drive much deeper connections.

- **Be consistent**—I use the expression, "Never too high, never too low." First off, the highs are never as good as you think they are, and the lows are never as bad. When you are viewing a low as something really bad, ask yourself if it will induce the same level of anxiety in a year. If the answer is no, which it often is, don't overreact. Practicing consistent messaging leads to credibility, respect, and trust.

- **Be honest**—On countless occasions, I have seen leaders cloak poor results in order to appear successful. While we want to find the good in all situations, it is important to be open about both the good and the bad. If your team misses its goal, tell the members that they missed, and share the expectations for the future. Open and honest communication must not be filtered. In filtering, we are sidestepping the "honest" part of "open and honest." The message itself will be tailored for the audience, understanding and being sensitive to how the listeners will hear it, but the point is that we have to practice honesty in order to be transparent. In order to improve, we must know where we have fallen short. Share your belief in the team, but be sure to share the misses as well.

- **Be unique**—Practice varied communication approaches. Instead of e-mail, send video messages weekly. Some video messages can be status updates, while others can be fun and even self-deprecating. Do fireside chats. Sing a song, lip-sync, do something silly. Being unique keeps people guessing and allows them to see you in a different light.
- **Be inclusive**—Find time for everyone. Schedule time to speak with members of your team individually, even if it's just to touch base or say hello. Meet them in person for a coffee, or videoconference with them and have a virtual lunch together.
- **Team communication**—Set team goals and share them openly. People want to know what they are shooting for, and they want to win as part of a team. They want to set new highs. They want to break records. Be aggressive in team goal setting, and you will be pleasantly surprised more often than not. Provide consistent personal and team updates, as well as anticipated needs of the business.
- **Individual communication**—Recognize people individually and in group settings. People love recognition, and once that foundation and expectation has been cast as a standard, they will work hard to achieve at a recognition-worthy level. There is little that is more powerful in influencing your culture and results than consistent and genuine recognition, both individual and collective. Building a recognition-rich culture is an absolute imperative.
- **Take the temperature consistently**—There is no task more valuable than getting in the field and spending

time in front of clients and with your team. Set small group lunches with team members to gain their thoughts on pressing items. Survey the field. Entrust projects to committees. Give your employees a platform to be heard and to make an impact. Openly seek feedback.

- **Work on pronouns**—*We* over *they* and *us* over *them*. When a team member uses terms outside of *we* and *us*, be sure to make a point to stop them and ask, "Who are 'they'?" It will send an important message that you are building a team and that we speak in team terms.

Effective communication builds cohesive teams. Open communication allows for a platform of honesty, sincerity, and teamwork. Honest communication leads to a culture of trust and support. Commit to creating a recognition-rich culture, and rewards will result. The team will follow the leader's path. Communication and recognition begin at the top and permeate through the entire organization. A culture of transparency and openness allows the leader to explain the *why* when making tough decisions or announcements. Teams will accept both the good and the bad from a leader whom they know has their best interests and the interests of the organization at heart. By consistently practicing open, honest, and genuine communication, you will create not only a team that will flourish in good times but one that will also weather the tough times, standing side by side and not running for the exits.

CLOSE

When writing a book, authors are consistently asked two questions: "What's your book about?" and "How long did it take you to write it?" Allow me to answer the second question first and close by addressing the first question last.

In April 1986, I assumed my first true leadership role. I recall the day vividly. I was promoted to lead an inside sales team of thirty-five professionals. Having found success in sales, I was hopeful that I would be able to translate my sales skills to leadership and help others achieve their potential and beyond. I was driven to help others and through their successes, I found my passion and my calling. Through a myriad of successes, challenges, failures, tough love, and great mentorship, I learned what I share with you today. This book is a compilation of firsthand teachings and learnings, bumps and bruises, successes and failures, joys and tears. So I guess you could say that I started writing this book on the day I was granted my first opportunity to lead.

As for the theme of this book, I wanted to go deep into the four areas of every business that drive results, build amazing cultures, and create something truly special. When we focus on our people, their/our passions, our organization's proposition, and the process by which everything moves fluidly, we put ourselves in a position to have our organization feel more like a family than a business. It is a rare feat to reach this level, but knowing your levers and pulling them will lead you to that point. It takes work. It also takes full commitment and daily focus, built around the right mission and the right people. We've covered a lot of ground in *Pulling Levers*—likely more than a leader can fully consume. Thus, I want to close by capturing the twenty-five most relevant points. These points are the foundation of *Pulling Levers*:

- **Stand for something**—Put stakes in the ground around your beliefs. Commit to that which drives you, and share it openly. Leave no doubt about what is important to you (success of your people, creating a "best place to work," etc.).
- ***You* control the fate of your culture**—While every employee has a direct hand in the makeup of an organization's culture, the leader sets the tone and influences the outcome above all others. Pour yourself into your culture, and embody all that it stands for, as your team will follow your lead.
- **Make hiring *great* people your top priority**—Every bit of your organizational success will come as a result of the character and talent of those whom you allow to be a part of your team. One misalignment can influence the entire environment. Be involved in

every aspect of recruitment, onboarding, training, and employee development. Hire people with good hearts who are grateful, humble, outwardly focused, passionate, and driven.

- **Never settle for less than A**—You cannot expect A-level performance from C-level players. If an employee has the will to succeed, work on his or her skill, and help him or her achieve A status. There is room for solid Bs who fit culturally and contribute passionately. There is no room for C performers.

- **Fail fast**—We have all made mistakes in hiring. The sooner you own up to it, the better. Don't allow the situation to fester or drag out. Be respectful yet decisive when it comes to talent. You will be judged based on your action or inaction on performance issues. Move swiftly when it comes to talent. Your results and culture depend on it.

- **Create a living, breathing value system**—Brainstorm, develop, agree on, and articulate your corporate values. Build these values as a team. By authoring the value system together, you will own it together. Post your corporate values everywhere, and openly recognize those employees who embody your values monthly or quarterly. Give out awards or trophies that can be displayed for all to see. With consistent and solid reinforcement comes a deep value system, complete with acknowledgement, acceptance, and passion through ownership.

- **Re-create yourself and your organization**—You and your company are works in progress. Never forget that. In order to keep the environment fresh and alive, work to keep your culture in the "dating" stage. Bring new ideas forward. Be open to feedback and suggestions. Create a culture that allows for creative thinking. Avoid the comfort trap, as this will lead to boredom and complacency. Build a culture accepting of change and open to re-creation.

- **Tell your story passionately**—Whether speaking of your personal or professional self, tell your story with great emotion and authentic passion. People want to be associated with leaders who exude positivity, embody values, and share their beliefs openly and genuinely.

- **Build a culture of transparency**—Make it your mission to develop an open culture void of secrets and drama. Build an involved culture in which opinions matter and involvement is expected. Share financial information, successes, and failures.

- **Entrust key decisions to others**—Build committees to address challenges and opportunities. Present tough problems to smart people, and allow them to develop solutions. You will likely settle at a better spot than you would had you solved the issue yourself, while also building an involved culture and witnessing the development of future leaders of your organization.

- **Establish a recognition-rich culture**—Through compensation, words, and actions, commit to recognizing and celebrating achievement. Develop fun and themed incentives, and share updates consistently. Take time to send thank-you cards and gifts to spouses, thanking them for allowing the company to "borrow" their partners. Every day, send a personal note to at least one employee, recognizing something that he or she did well that moved the organization forward.

- **Understand and articulate your** *why*—Employees and clients buy the *why*, not the *how* or the *what*. Focus on your company's *why*, and call for all employees to internalize the uniqueness of the proposition, the problem that it solves, and the opportunity that it creates for others.

- **Know and attack your KPIs**—Mission first. Vision second. Values third. Expectations fourth. Build KPIs that will lead to overdelivery of expectations and satisfy the values, vision, and mission of the organization. Articulate KPIs by division and role, aligning compensation to KPIs.

- **Commit to the process**—A successful organization understands and openly communicates the expectations and standards that are central to its processes. Standards are the minimum-accepted expectations that must be met by all employees. Standards are the executable and controllable "bite-size chunks" of the KPIs. For a process to be embraced, it must begin with the actions and commitment of senior leaders.

- **Overhire recruiters**—Not just recruiters, but great recruiters. In order to topgrade effectively, identifying and engaging A-level talent requires A-level recruiters. Get out ahead of your recruitment efforts.

- **Commit to your culture**—Hire great people, and allow them to contribute to the greater good of the organization. Fundamentally focus on connecting your employees to your mission, vision, and values, while providing opportunities that challenge them and allow them to advance and to be compensated appropriately. Commit to employee development, and truly value employees' input and contributions. If you're committed to hiring A players, get out of their way and let them do what they do best. Engaged employees stay. Invest in your employees first, and they will invest in relationships with their clients.

- **Prioritize onboarding**—Make new employees' first day an event. Blow away your new candidates by helping them feel amazing about their decision to join your company. Go out of your way to confirm that they made the right decision. Involve the entire company in welcoming new employees, as these new folks will either advance your culture or hinder it.

- **Invest in training**—Bring aboard the best, brightest, and most passionate people to share your vision, and commit to new hires' success. Look for people with an outward focus and a passion for developing others. Pay them well, and hold them accountable for meeting the ramp expectations of new employees. Tie their compensation to the new employees' goal achievement, and they will ensure success.

- **Identify the best, learn what they do, and share it**—Leverage the talent within your organization to ensure success for all. Focus your efforts on understanding what the best people do, and build training and streamline processes around that. Make your best people ambassadors of your business, clearly articulating what they do and mentoring others to follow their lead. The mightiest impact is felt when peers teach peers.

- **Pay for performance**—Implement a compensation plan that severely overpays the best people, as they will stretch and will stay as a result of feeling valued and well compensated. Underpay for poor performance, and make no apologies for it. In a success-driven organization, leaders must stretch their people to achieve more than they believed possible. When they do, pay them really well.
- **Align compensation to organizational KPIs**—In order for a compensation plan to more than pay for itself, every role must align with the needs of the business. Leader compensation must be aligned with that of their people, and vice versa. Compensation plans break down when there are competing goals. Focus everyone at all levels on the KPIs that will drive organizational success.
- **Embrace metrics**—Become a metrics-driven organization. Focus and make changes based on data, avoiding gut decisions. Remember, you can't manage what you can't measure. The data will shape the path. Data doesn't lie. The answer is in the numbers. Bring visibility to every aspect of the business by implementing an analytical approach to your operation.
- **Rank people**—The only way to commit to having a team made up of A players is to clearly understand who they are. Rankings provide visibility of the metrics important to the role and the business. Rankings will move your business and allow top performers to view their successes. Rankings motivate top players to reach higher levels.
- **Realize the impact you have on the company**—As a leader, understand the responsibility you personally

have to the culture and the success of your organization. Your team will take on your persona and will flex as you flex. Commit to your people and their success above all else. When those you serve win, your clients and your organization win.

- **Positivity always**—Committed employees spend a lot of time together. The choice to create a positive environment falls squarely on your shoulders. Find the joy within, and spread that among your people. Your people, your clients, and your organization are relying on you to lead by example and through a positive spirit and outward drive to serve and win. Commit to creating a positive environment built on the core values of trust, respect, integrity, and kindness. Focus on doing well by doing good for others.